OPTIONS TRADING CRASH COURSE

Quick Start Guide For Beginners To Learn Risk And Reward. Overcome Fear And Anxiety In Stock Market Investing Through The Best Passive Income Strategies.

George Greek

Table of Contents

Introduction

Options trading can be daunting for those with little to no experience, but it doesn't have to be. Options are a simple tool that allows you to increase your returns on investments and leverage the power of buying low and selling high.

In this article, we'll explore the basics of options trading so that you can start to educate yourself about how they work. We'll talk about what they are, the different types and when you might use them.

What Are Options?

There are many ways to make money in the stock market. You can buy a stock outright, you can short sell stocks and you could even trade options. The first thing you need to understand about options is that they are contracts that give the buyer the right to buy or sell a stock at a specific price before a specific date. Call Options are the right to buy stocks at a predetermined price and Put Options are the right to sell stocks at a predetermined price. There is a buyer and a seller for every option and the seller is obligated to fulfill the contract the buyer should choose to exercise it.

If you're using options as a way to trade stocks, a put option is basically insurance against losing money. If you own stocks and fear they might drop in value, you can buy put option contracts to protect the stocks from losing too much. If the stocks don't drop, you don't have to do anything else and your put option expires worthless. If the stock drops below the strike price, you can sell your stocks at the predetermined price and then buy them back with the option contract. That way you avoid losing money on your original investment. If you're looking to trade options as an investment strategy on its own, then buying call option contracts is a good way to do it. If you think a stock is going to go up in value, you can buy call option contracts with a strike price that's higher than the current market price. That way you can make money if the stock goes up. If the stock doesn't go up, your option expires worthless and you lose the money that you paid for it. Your goal in that situation would be to buy the stocks at the strike price and then sell them for a higher price. Options are a great way to trade stocks or build your investment portfolio.

Types of Options

There are two main types of options: equity and index.

Equity options are the rights to buy a specific stock at a specific price in the future. Index options are rights to buy or sell an entire index, like the S&P 500. You can also trade options on futures contracts, which are agreements to buy or sell a specific commodity at a specific price in the future.

These are known as futures options but they work in similar ways to equity and index options.

You can also trade options on currency pairs. Instead of buying the US dollar or any other currency, you can buy options on the exchange rate between two currencies. In this case, the underlying asset is currencies and not stocks.

Using Options in Your Portfolio

One of the great things about options trading is that it lets you take a more active role in your portfolio. If you have stocks that are performing poorly but you still think they have the potential to go up, you can buy put option contracts to protect your investment. This way you don't have to sell your stocks and take a loss, giving them a second chance to go up in value. Buying put option contracts is also a great way to hedge your portfolio.

If you have stocks that are doing well but you're afraid that they might have a correction, you can buy put option contracts to protect your portfolio. If the stocks don't drop in value, you don't have to do anything and your put option contracts expire worthlessly. If your stocks do drop in value, the put option contracts allow you to sell your stocks at the predetermined price and then buy them back with the option contract. This way you can avoid losing money on your original investment. You can do it too!

Options trading can seem like a daunting task, but it doesn't have to be. It can be a simple way to trade stocks or the underlying assets of futures contracts. You can start by reading up on the basics of options and learning how they work. This way you can get a better idea of how they can work for you and how to use them. You don't have to dive right into the deep end, especially if you're just starting out. The best way to learn how to swim is to step into the shallow end and slowly wade into the deeper water. This will give you time to get comfortable with the process and then gradually build up your confidence.

Hopefully, by now you have a solid understanding of options trading. You don't have to use them on your own or as part of an active trading strategy. You can use options as a way to build your investment portfolio, protect your investments, and work towards meeting your goals.

You can also use options to trade stocks. Whatever you decide to do with them, having a solid understanding of options trading will help you make the right decision for yourself.

Chapter 1. Master the Basic Nuts and Bolts of Options Trading (Buy or Sell Calls and Puts)

Buying and Selling Puts

Let's talk about buying and selling puts. Puts, of course, allow you to sell the stock that you have or the underlying commodity that you have underneath it all. There are different reasons why people may want to buy or sell puts, and here we'll go over what it is, how to do it, and the advantages of such.

What is Buying and Selling Puts?

Selling/buying puts essentially is giving someone the option to buy the stock at a certain amount of money.

If you sell a put option, you're selling the chance for someone to buy that stock at a price.

If you buy a put option, you're giving someone the option to buy that stock for that price and the person is obligated to sell it.

So, let's say that you're planning on getting a put option to buy that stock at a certain amount of money. You can put that option down, and from there, wait for it to fall, and from there you can exercise it. Maybe you want to buy shares from a really good railroad company. You essentially notice it's increasing the earnings on this, and you decide to buy the stock when it's below 30 potentially. By buying a put option, it basically makes the seller obligated to sell you the stock when it falls below 30 dollars.

You want to exercise these in falling markets since you'll generate a profit when the market is falling, rather than rising.

Selling Puts in this Market

Here's the thing, when you want to sell puts, you should only do so if you're comfy with owning a stock that's under its actual price, because essentially, you're assuming the obligation to buy it if the person does decide to sell. From this, you should also only enter trades where the net price paid for the security is good. This is the most important part of selling puts profitably in the markets that you have. There are other reasons to sell it to the person. You can also own the security below the market price that is currently there, and you'll definitely want to be careful when you do choose to sell this.

An Example of Buying a Put

Let's now move onto buying these puts. One thing to note is that you're not going to see the commissions, taxes, margins, and other charges factored into any of these equations for a reason. That starts to get it a bit more complicated, and right now, we are just showing you the cut and dry of all of the ways you can buy a put option that can be considered. But you should definitely consult with your tax advisor or broker before you go in.

So, let's say you've got company A, which is overvalued currently at $50 bucks a share, and you decide to bet on a decline at this point, getting a put contract that's at $35 a share, and it costs $2 per share, so the "breakeven" price is $33 a share. This is deduced from basic math since you're taking the contract price of 35 minus the 2 making it $33 for this. Since each of these represents 100 different shares. That's $3500 in total of what you'll buy, and then of course it'll cost you upfront $200 for this (cause of the options contract and the shares) and from there, you enter the trade. Now, let's say that the option contract is for August 2019, and from there, you fast-forward and watch the market. Below is a table of what can happen.

Action of stock	What happens to you	Your return	Outlook
Soars all the way up to $60	The option expires, becomes worthless, and you lose the $200 premium, but you're basically losing nothing else	(0%)	Okay
Falls slightly to $38	Same thing happens, stock falls but you don't make a profit	(0%)	Okay
Drops all the way to $25	You make some cash! 800 dollars to be exact ($35-25) and then the $2 premium	(800%)	Nice!

Drops to $0 (basically going bankrupt)	The ideal situation, and you'll get $3300 from it (0 at expiration, so 3500-200 from the premium)	(1500%)	Ideal!

So, the best time to use these is when you have a sinking ship in terms of stock. Otherwise, they aren't worth your time, and it's better not to have these stocks, and there is always a chance you could end up losing money. But, if the person sells the stock, and you turn around and cash in on it, you'll have more money, and you don't have to worry about the burden of a stock.

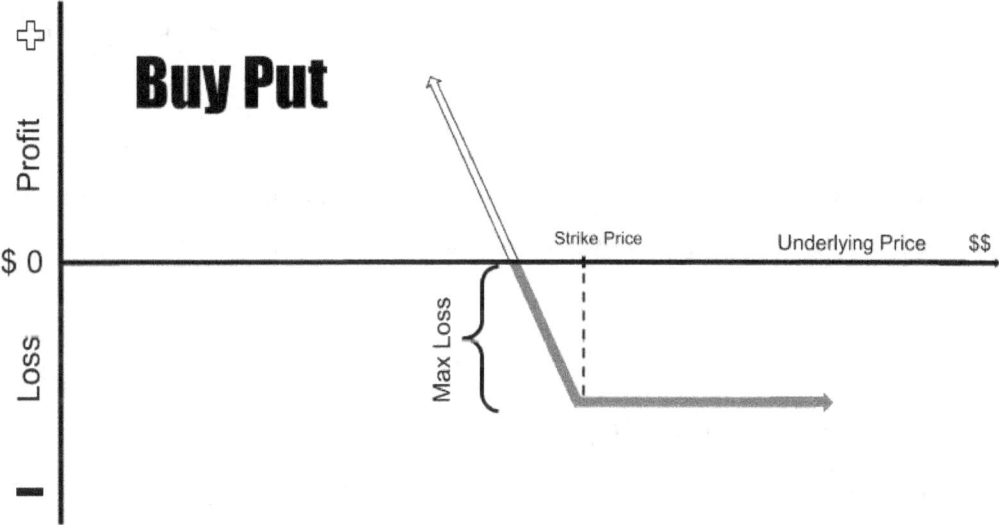

If you choose to buy it when it declines, you're essentially going to get money from this. You want to do it when it's declining and nothing more. It is very important that you don't choose to act on these types of options until it's that time.

That's it, that's all buying put options is, and you want to make sure that it falls to the level that you want it to be at.

The risks of It

Risks are still there in both cases. Options are risky due to the complex nature of this, but once you know how this works, it can reduce the risk a whole lot. Put options, in particular, can be quite risky, especially for the seller, since they may have to spend more money buying back the option that they once had.

One other aspect of this, especially for buyers, is the break-even aspects of it. So, let's assume that you got a stock today for $46 and this was at $44, which is two points down of what it actually is, so you'll be profitable in the trade. But, here's the thing, you're going to end up losing out on money due to the fee for the option. It would make the option worth $2 since you spent $4 on it, so that means you're losing out on it.

But there is also the fact that if the option does expire and you're in-the-money, you'll get the right stock immediately. You may not realize it, but these can be quite good, especially for plunging markets, if you know they will bounce back.

If you end up seeing it goes high, you're going to end up paying for that premium to get the right to buy it, and that's money that can rack up to a couple of thousand dollars. Do make sure that you understand that when you do choose to figure out your own stock, and how you can easily rectify.

The Advantages of Buying Puts

Buying puts, which gives you an option to sell the stock at a given price, is good if you're looking to protect yourself. So, let's say that you have this stock, or you've been eyeing a stock that will probably fall, and then rise over the next few months. There are those out there, and usually, it's due to lulls in the market at the time. So, you decide to buy the put that's there, which gives you the option to sell that stock when the market decides to resurface at a higher level.

For you, you're taking a gamble on this, because the market may not recover, but if you notice a stock that could potentially have the power to fall, this may be a good one. That way, you can get the stock for cheaper. From there, you can sell the stock again, and you have the right to sell that stock at the price you're looking for.

It essentially allows you to form that extra security in it, which is a nice little advantage for the person who wants to sell it. Long puts are good for this, especially if you want to sell these.

Put options let you sell this asset at the strike price that's there. With this, the seller is then obligated to purchase these shares from the holder. Now, how can this help? Let's say that you buy a stock at 20 bucks, and then you compare it to 20 dollars at the actual edge. If the price is below 20 at any point, you can actually then exercise the options and reduce the losses. This can definitely help, especially if you're willing to buy an option, and from there, sell it in order to avoid lots of trouble.

Naked Puts

There are also naked puts, which is an advanced put options strategy, so I don't suggest trying this till you've worked with basic puts. The reason for that is they're incredibly risky.

What does it mean to trade an option naked though? It doesn't mean that you're going to the stock exchange in the buff, but rather, you're selling the options without having a position in the underlying instrument. For example, if you're writing a naked put, you're selling a put without having the stock.

The covered call is probably the most basic stock trading strategy. This strategy provides an ideal entry point for those who are new to options trading and allows them to turn their existing investment activities into a gateway for trading options. The premise of the covered call is quite simple. The idea behind this strategy is to minimize your cost basis on your stock purchases.

Let's take a look at how this works.

Other Considerations

The biggest income generator in this strategy is the time value that's built into the option. Consider this: Let's say we stick with the 1270 strike, but play around with the expiration date. What are the premiums we would earn for strike dates that are closer than the one on October 25th?

Well, the calls expiring on September 20th, which is less than a week away, will yield you a princely sum of $0.19. September 27th will yield you $1.40. Things get a little better in October. October 4th gives us $4.80. October 11th nets us $6.90 and finally, October 18th, which is about a week apart from our choice of October 25th, will yield us $9.91.

So, a difference of a week results in a premium decrease from $16 to $9.91. That's a 38% price drop! Hopefully, now you can see my point about the value of time decay. It decreases exponentially and thus you should take full advantage of it. If time decay decreases exponentially, surely it makes sense to pick an expiry date that is as far away as possible? Well, let's see how this plays out.

Chapter 2. Understand the Theory and Mathematics Behind Options

Options theory is a branch of mathematics that deals with modeling and analyzing uncertainty. The idea behind options theory is to find ways to make the best possible choice under conditions of uncertainty. The theories and mathematics behind options theory are not easy to understand, but this article will help you get started.

Furthermore, the writer or seller of the option has the obligation to sell (in case of a call option) or buy (in the case of a put option) the asset if requested by the buyer. The price of buying an option is called the premium; it represents the maximum possible loss of the option buyer. The premium is paid by the buyer to the seller when the option contract is signed.

For example, a call option for 100 shares of IBM with a strike price of $100 and a premium of $3 will cost the buyer $300. As the writer of the option has to buy (or sell) the asset if requested by the holder, he or she is exposed to unlimited potential loss.

The seller of an option is short on the option. The writer's potential loss is limited to the premium received, whereas the buyer's potential loss is theoretically unlimited. The buyer of the option has unlimited potential gain and the seller of the option has a limited potential gain. The writer of an option is long the asset, in this case, IBM stock.

The buyer of an option is short on the option. A put option gives the buyer of the option a right to sell from the writer of the option at a preset price. A call option is therefore negative leverage on an underlying asset, while a put option is positive leverage.

The seller of a call option is long on the underlying asset. The seller of a put option is short on the underlying asset. The investor has the right to buy 100 shares from IBM at $100 per share. In this example, the buyer of the option has unlimited potential gain (theoretically) and the seller of the option has a limited potential gain. The seller of a call option receives an up-front premium.

The options' main application is to hedge the risk of holding an asset. For example, an investor may hold a stock portfolio worth $9 million. The investor is concerned that the market will move against his portfolio and reduce its value by 25%. The investor buys four call options on his stock portfolio. Each option gives the investor the right to buy 100 shares of his own stock portfolio. At the same time, the investor sells four call options on his stock portfolio to a bank. Each option gives the bank the right to buy 100 shares of his own stock portfolio from him. The investor is left with a portfolio worth $9 million and no obligations. If the market moves against him, he can buy back the options and be left with his initial $9 million. In this example, the buyer of the options has unlimited potential gain and the seller of the options has a limited potential loss.

Example of a put option: An investor is worried about some but not all stocks in his portfolio. He buys 10 put options for $3 each. Each option gives him the right, but not an obligation, to sell 100 shares of stock at $100 per share. If the market moves against some of these stocks, he can buy the options back and be left with a portfolio worth $9 million. He will have lost $300 by buying the put options. In this example, the buyer of the options has unlimited potential loss while the seller of the options has a limited potential gain.

Options theory is used in several industries including banking, insurance, energy, transportation and information technology. Options theory has been used to make critical decisions in these industries, such as whether to participate in the financial markets or not. In banking, options theory is used to determine the best route for a bank's portfolio. If a bank is long on the asset, in this case, the stock also needs to be short on the option. The bank will receive an up-front premium for writing the option. If the value of the bank's stock increases, the bank can buy back the option and be left with a portfolio worth $9 million. If the value of the bank's stock decreases, the bank can buy back the options and be left with its original $9 million.

Chapter 3. What Are the Factors That Affect Options Pricing?

Alternatives costs are resolved to a limited extent by the cost of the underlying stock.

Be that as it may, options costs are also impacted when left to termination and some different elements. We will go over the various ways that the cost of a given option can change and what will be behind the changes. It's critical to have a sturdy handle of these ideas, so you don't go into choices as a gullible starting dealer.

The Market Price of Shares

The most significant factor that impacts the cost of an option is the cost of the speculation known as the stock that is behind the option. Be that as it may, it is anything but a 1-1 relationship. The measure of impact from the hidden stock is going to change with time. Moreover, it relies upon whether the option is in the money, at the money, or out of the money. The portion of the value of the option that is dependent on the cost of the underlying stock is known as the estimation of the appropriate option.

If an option can be equivalent to the market evaluating or not be relatively preferred, it has zero intrinsic worth. An option would need to be evaluated in the money to have any inherent worth.

For a call option, if the market cost is lower than the strike cost or the equivalent, the choice will have no estimating at all from the inherent worth. On the off chance that the offer cost is higher than the value used to exchange shares employing the option, the option will have inherent worth.

For a put option, if the offer cost is at or over the strike value, the option will have zero intrinsic worth. If the offer cost is beneath the strike value, at that point, the alternative will have some incentive from the stock. This is called intrinsic worth.

In any case, to confound matters, when an option is at or out of the money, the cost of the hidden stock has some impact that can change the estimation of option. The measure of the impact that the market cost of the thing known as the stock has on the cost of the option is given by an amount that is called delta. You can peruse the incentive for delta by taking a look at the information for any option that you are keen on exchanging. It is a decimal worth running from 0 to 1 for call options, and it's given as a negative incentive for put options.

The explanation given for a negative reason for put options is this mirrors the way that if the stock cost increases, the cost of a put option will decrease. Conversely, if the stock cost decreases, the estimation of the put option will increment. It's an inverse relationship, and along these lines, the delta is negative for put options.

To see how this will play out, how about we take a look at a particular model. Assume that we have a $100 choice. That is, the strike cost is set to $100. If the cost of the underlying stock is $105, delta for the call option is 0.77.

That implies that if the dollar estimates the stock increments by $1, the estimation of an option will ascend by around 77 pennies. This is for every offer value change. In this way, for the option that you are exchanging, there are 100 fundamental offers. Along these lines, a 77-penny cost rise would build the estimation of the option by $77.

For a put option with a similar strike value, the choice would be out of the money, because the offer cost is higher than the strike cost. For this situation, for the put option, the delta is given as - 0.23. That implies that the put option would lose roughly $23 if the offer cost went up by $1. If the offer cost dropped by $1, the put option would pick up $23.

The inborn estimation of the call option portrayed in this hypothetical exercise would be $5 per share. The total expense of the option would be $6.06 per share, mirroring the way that the call option has $1.06 in extraneous worth. Conversely, the put option has zero inherent worth. It has nearly the equivalent outward worth, be that as it may, at $1.03.

I have utilized 45 days before lapsing for this activity. Numerical recipes administer alternatives costs, so it's conceivable to make assessments of what the option cost will be early. There are many numbers of crunchers and spreadsheets that are accessible for free online for this reason.

Now, suppose that instead, the offer cost was $95, with the goal that the call option was out of the money, and the put option was in the money. For this situation, the call option has zero intrinsic worth, and it has a $0.94 outward worth with the goal that the option would be worth $94. Delta has changed, but not actually. For this situation, for the call option, the delta is 0.25.

On the off chance that the offer value rose to $96, with everything else unaltered, the cost of the call option would ascend to $1.21 per share. This represents you can even now acquire profits from less expensive out of the money options.

If the offer cost remained at $95, the put option would have a delta of - 0.75. Notice that if we take the total worth and include the delta for the call and the put option, they summarize to 1.0.

In this way, on the off chance that you see a call option with a strike that is lower than the market cost, with a delta given by state 0.8, that implies the put option with a similar strike cost. The termination date will have a delta of -0.20.

Delta accomplishes more than give you the expectation of changes in the essential offer cost and value developments of the alternative. Likewise, it gives you a (harsh) gauge of the likelihood to end in the money for the agreement known as a choice.

On the off chance that you offer to open, you don't need the alternative to lapse in the money. Subsequently, you are most likely going to sell alternatives that have a little delta. If you purchase to open, you need the alternative to go in the money, on the off chance that it isn't now. In this way, you would purchase an alternative with a higher delta.

If we state that a given call option has a delta of 0.66, this shows on the off chance that we see changes to such an extent that the fundamental stock value ascends by $1, the cost of the choice on a for-each-offer premise will ascend by $0.66. In any case, it likewise reveals to us that there is a 66% possibility that this choice will end in a favorable condition: it will be in the money.

Something different you have to know is that delta is dynamic. If the cost of offer increments available, delta ascends for the call option and gets littler in size for the put option. A declining share cost will have the contrary impact.

The sum that delta will change is given by another "Greek"—gamma. Most starting dealers presumably won't be too stressed over gamma; what we've depicted so far is, in reality, all you have to know to go into fruitful alternatives exchanges. In any case, gamma will reveal the variation in the estimation of delta with an adjustment in stock cost. Thus, if gamma is 0.03, this implies a $1 ascend in the stock cost will build delta by 0.03 for a call option. The reverse relationship holds for a put option.

If a choice is at the money, the delta will be about 0.50 for a call option and -0.50 for a put option. That bodes well if the strike cost is equivalent to the offer cost available. There is a half likelihood that the market cost will move beneath the strike cost, and there is a half likelihood that the market offers' cost will move over the strike cost.

Implied Volatility

One of the most significant attributes of choices in the wake of considering delta and time decay is the sum a stock cost changes with time. Instability will give you a thought of in what capacity the value of the stock will swing. On the off chance that you take a look at a stock graph, I am confident that you are accustomed to seeing the cost go all over a great deal, giving a great sudden turn. The more it varies, and the greater the vacillations in value, the higher the unpredictability.

Everything is relative. Thus, you can't state that any stock has a "flat out" level of unpredictability. What happens is the unpredictability for the whole market is determined. Afterward, the instability of a stock is contrasted with the instability of the market all in all. When taking a look at the stocks themselves, this is given by an amount called beta.

If the stock, for the most part, moves with the financial exchange everywhere, beta is safe. On the off chance that beta is 1.0, it implies that it has a similar instability as the whole market. That is a stock with normal unpredictability.

If beta is under 1.0, at that point, the stock doesn't have a lot of instability. A sum beneath 1.0 shows you how considerably less unpredictable the stock is in contrast with the market in general. Along these lines, if the beta is given as 0.7, it implies the stock is 30% less unpredictable than the typical market.

On the off chance that beta is higher than 1.0, at that point, the stock is more unstable than normal. If you see a stock with a beta of 1.42, it implies the stock is 42% more unstable than the normal for the market.

Move against the market. At the point when the market goes up, it goes down and the other way around. Most stocks don't have a negative beta. However, they are not hard to track down either.

Instability is a robust amount. When you find it, you are taking a look at a preview of the unpredictability at that given second. Obviously, under most conditions, it's not liable to change, particularly over brief timeframe periods like half a month or a month. There are exceptional cases to this, including profit season.

Suggested instability is an amount that is given for choices. Suggested instability is a proportion of the certain unpredictability that the stock cost is required to see over the lifetime of an option (that is until the expiry date).

Chapter 4. How Are Options Different Than Stocks

There is a big difference between options trading and stock trading.

Stock represents partial ownership of the company implying that when you purchase a stock, you are normally a part of the company. The market may be so volatile but the strike prices reads are so high, and when the market activities are depicted to be calm, the strike prices may eventually be so down.

Let us look at some of the major differences between options trading and stock trading:

- Options derive the actual value from the value of the other assets involved during options trading, whereas stocks have a definite actual value that is fully recognized by the company in question.

- In the options trading activities, traders just have the full rights of the value amount. On the other hand, stock trading gives the traders full ownership of the property involved during trading activities.

- In options trading, the market predictability does not necessarily depend on the rates of supply and demand levels as compared to stock trading. With this in mind, the options trader is unlikely to predict what happens to the market but he/she can, however, check on the volatility of the market.

- Options are much cheaper than stock. Money is so fundamental in trading and is always the biggest motivation in any kind of trading activity. Options are less expensive since the trader gets to acquire 100 shares of the equity during trading. Moreover, the cost of grasping an option contract is much cheaper as compared to purchasing and the underlying stock, and the trader acquires more benefits as compared to stock trading.

- Options are normally a great leverage tool in maximizing the amounts of profits gained during a particular trading period as compared to stock trading. This is evident in the collection of various amounts of premiums during the issuance of contracts hence increasing the amounts of profits collected in options trading as compared to stock trading.

- Options trading is much good at flexibility as compared to stock trading as evident in its tactical operations that happen frequently in various trading activities. Traders can make smaller investments that lead to good amounts of profits and fewer risks involved during a particular period. On the other hand, stock trading calls for good investments with multiple amounts of risks over an unspecified period.

- Another point is that options have a great chance of limiting the risks that are likely to be involved during trading, as compared to stock trading, where risk is pretty much unlimited during the unspecified period of trading.

- Options trading can better for you if your timing is okay, and as an options trader, you will be able to acquire larger amounts of profits during the contract as compared to when you would be involved in options trading.

- Options trading allows a particular option trader to bet where the market will not go—an activity that is not allowed in stock trading. The advantage of this opportunity is that there are higher chances of success than betting on where the market will go.

Chapter 5. How You Can Use Options Even If You Invest in Stocks and Create Superior Combo Strategies

When it comes to portfolio diversity and the endless possibilities of options trading, there are countless ways to create a strategy that will serve you well in the long-run. A popular option trading strategy that we at Ally Invest are seeing more of is the combo strategy. A combo strategy is when a trader invests in stocks and options at the same time. Combos are accomplished by purchasing a call or put option for an underlying stock while simultaneously owning the underlying stock itself. The idea behind creating a combo trade is to reduce risk while still offering a profit opportunity. Using these strategies, the investor will be able to limit his or her risk on the stock as well as enjoy the option's time decay. It is important to note that the investor still has the potential of profit by purchasing a call or put option. We have outlined a few examples below to show you how you can use options even if you invest in stocks.

Combo Strategy #1: Inverse ETF and Stock Combo

This combo strategy involves owning a put or call option on an inverse ETF while also investing in the underlying stock of that particular ETF. Inverse ETFs are designed to move in the opposite direction of an underlying index. For example, if the S&P 500 is up 1%, then the inverse ETF should be down 1%. This particular combo strategy has a lot of profit potential because the stock price will continue to move down since the investor is shorting the underlying stock. On the other hand, the investor's investment in the ETF is covered by the call or put option. This limits your risk in case the stock unexpectedly rises.

Combo Strategy #2: Stock and Inverse ETF Combo

Investors can also use the inverse ETF and stock combo strategy while owning just the underlying stock. This is a great strategy for investors looking to maximize profit potential. The idea behind this strategy is to take advantage of the ETF's inverse movement while also having the option's time decay on your side. The investor will profit from the option's time decay while observing the ETF's inverse movement.

The profit and loss potential with this strategy is unlimited. For example, if the underlying stock is up 10%, then the ETF should be down 10% or more.

This combo strategy can be very rewarding for investors looking to generate a high profit.

Combo Strategy #3: Stock and Long Call Combo

A stock and long call combo strategy is a great way to maximize your profit potential when you own shares in a stock.

This strategy involves purchasing one call option for every 100 shares of the underlying stock.

For example, if you own 1000 shares of the stock, then you should purchase 10 call options with 10 different exercise prices.

This strategy is advantageous because the investor can take advantage of the option's time decay while also seeing the share price increase. Combos offer a lot of great diversity to an investor's portfolio. There are countless ways to create a combo strategy that will work for you.

As long as you take advantage of time decay as well as the potential movement of the underlying stock, you will be able to create a strategy that fits your needs.

Chapter 6. The Art of Adjusting Single Options Strategies

There are a number of different strategies that investors can implement for adjusting Single Option Strategies. This is the most popular adjustment strategy, which is typically referred to as "Delta-neutral." This strategy will be contrasted with other popular adjustments and the advantages and disadvantages of each. After reading this post, you should have a good understanding of the most common adjustment strategies that are used for single options. The information contained within this post is intended to be used by financial professionals. It should not be construed as investment advice, nor is it a solicitation to buy or sell any securities.

Delta

A delta is a measure of how much an option's price will change based on a 1-point move in the underlying stock. A delta of 0.50 means that the option's price will move 50 cents for each dollar move in the stock. The Delta-neutral strategy will attempt to maintain a position that has no directional exposure (i.e. no net directional exposure, or "no net delta"). A Delta-neutral position will have a positive and negative delta. In a Delta-neutral position, an increase in the underlying stock will cause a decrease in the net delta, and a decrease in the underlying stock will cause an increase in net delta. A Delta-neutral position will have no net directional exposure, and will be able to profit from increases in the underlying stock, while limiting losses on short option positions if the underlying stock decreases. As an example, if a trader wanted to create a Delta-neutral position with 5 options, he could buy 1 option with a $5.00 strike and sell 4 options with the same $5.00 strike.

This would create a position that has no net directional exposure since the positions have opposite deltas. If the stock increased by $1.00, then the delta of the short options would increase by 0. The delta of the long option would decrease by 0.50, and the net delta of the position would decrease by 0.50. If the stock decreased by $1.00, then the delta of the short options would decrease by 0. The delta of the long option would increase by 0. The net delta of the position would increase by 0.50.

A position with no net directional exposure will have unlimited profit potential and limited risk potential. The unlimited profit potential comes from the fact that it has no directional exposure, and is therefore not subject to the "directional risk" that a directional option position faces. The limited risk potential comes from the fact that the losses are capped at 100% of the initial margin required to create the position. In other words, if the stock goes down by more than 100% of the initial margin required to create the position, then the losses will be exactly 100% of the initial margin.

If you think that the underlying stock will increase or decrease by more than 100%, then you should not create a Delta-neutral position with those options. Delta-neutral strategies typically require a large amount of initial margin, and this can be a disadvantage for the investor. In addition, Delta-neutral strategies tend to be difficult to implement. The reason for this is that it is not possible to simultaneously have no net directional exposure and no net delta.

Therefore, in order to create a Delta-neutral position, it is necessary to first create a directional position with a net delta, and then adjust the position in order to remove the net directional exposure. The adjustment process will typically involve buying or selling options with a different strike and then holding the position for a period of time in order to allow the changes in deltas to "settle" over time. In the example above, the first adjustment would involve buying or selling options with a different strike and then holding the position. The second adjustment would involve buying or selling options with a different strike and then holding the position.

By continually making adjustments, it is possible to eventually create a Delta-neutral position. There are a number of different adjustments that can be used, and many traders use a variety of different adjustments depending upon market conditions.

Chapter 7. Risk Management

Risk management includes defining, assessing, and prioritizing the threats or uncertainties and ensuring that the effect of threats is minimized, monitored, and managed or strengthened by the use of co-ordinate and economical tools.

For every organization, risk management is important. It provides foresight for investment returns and projects every potential setback for a company by starting a new (or even routine) effort.

Five steps must be taken first to evaluate the risk and the best solution before determining the most effective risk management strategy for your situation.

Identify the Risk

Risks include events that cause problems or advantages. Risk identification starts from the sources of domestic problems and benefits from competitors. Risks should be internal or external such that the program can be used to recognize the different possible risks.

Analyze the Risk

Once you have identified risks, the possible effects each has on consumer behavior, your business, and other current efforts can be analyzed thoroughly.

Evaluate the Risk

You can now allocate a rating quality to the likelihood of the results of each risk. This helps to explain how a project or new product is seriously threatened by a risk. You can also determine the extent to which each risk can destroy or support a new tactic. The magnitude is a combination of the probability and effect of the risk.

Treat the Risk

You will begin to handle the worst risks first, so you are conscious of all potential risks and their severity. First, you want to see if you can decrease the probability of a negative outcome and then how you can raise the chance. Prevention and contingency should be prepared at this stage in the risk assessment so that no surprises are found as you move forward with action plans.

Check the Risk

You know the threats, the probability, what happens if they happen, and how to avoid disasters. What next? Control the risks by monitoring the variables involved and proposing potential chain reaction hazards. As your system detects changes, treat the problem calmly to prevent large-scale onslaught effects, and to trigger a high risk.

It takes us to the next big risk management wave: risk control. There are several ways of treating risks, and they all depend on what kind of risks are addressed and how serious the effects or opportunities are. Let's look at the best strategies for treating the risk:

Evasion

Best case scenario, you can absolutely eliminate risk impacts. However, you also forfeit all risky activities, and all the associated potential returns and opportunities. What kind of dangerous operation you want to experiment with is up to you.

Reduction

Risk reduction introduces small changes to reduce both the weight of risk and the reward after the event. The reduction requires some process and plan manipulation, but in the event of a high-risk event, it saves your company from a serious loss.

Share

Risk-sharing or transfer redistributes over multiple parties the burden of loss or gain. These can include representatives of a corporation, an outsourced business, or an insurance policy.

Conservation

Danger retention implies the full expectation of loss or gain. This choice is better suited to small risks where losses can easily be sustained and compensated.

When we speak of risk, we refer to the possibility that an adverse event may arise and its consequences for us.

It must be made clear that since this concept is quite broad, we are only going to refer to financial risks, to explain how we can control those financial consequences that are negative for a business.

Types of Financial Risks

- Market risk: Associated with the variations suffered by the financial markets, and in which we can distinguish:
- Currency risk: they will be the consequence of the volatility of the currency market.
- Interest rate risk: they will be the consequence of the volatility of interest rates.
- Market risk: to refer more specifically to the volatility of the markets for financial instruments such as stocks, debt, derivatives, etc.
- Credit risk. One that refers to the possibility that one of the parties to a financial contract does not fulfill its contractual obligations.
- Liquidity or financing risk. It covers the fact that one of the parties to the financial contract cannot obtain the liquidity it needs to assume its obligations despite having assets (which it cannot sell) and the will to do so.
- Operational risk. The possibility of financial losses, whether due to a failure or insufficiency of processes, people, internal systems, technology, etc.

There are 3 ways to take a risk:

- Transfer the risk: We transfer the risk to another party, by selling that asset or by contacting an insurance policy.
- Evading risk: Simply do not expose yourself to the risk that has been identified.
- Retain the risk: We directly assume the risk, and we will have to make the decision of how we are going to cover the possible losses.

How to decrease your financial risk? Through Control and management.

This is one of the issues that entrepreneurs most often worry about when talking about the company's livelihood. And we fully understand that because the entire company could fall apart just by making a mistake.

For this reason, I'm going straight to the point, we have made a list, short but very useful, that will help you, if not to reduce, at least to be able to control and manage the risks that your company runs.

- **Evaluate the profitability of each investment**. This is something you should never forget. You have to always keep in mind that the more information you have about the operations, the lower the risk.

- **Anticipate the future.** We know that this is impossible, but referring to the previous point, we may get very close to what can happen later if we have great information to help us compare situations, decision-making, and strategies.
- **Diversify.** Something fundamental that can never be lacking in any risk control strategy is diversification. We can do this by proposing investments of various types, for example, highly dangerous investments that compensate for others of very low risk.
- **Having a professional team**. Managing your accounts deserves specialized knowledge of new financial trends. You can always protect some of your assets by taking out insurance.
- **The hedging**. Along the same lines as diversification, we can also combine some assets from the same portfolio, with the aim that the variations of some counterbalance those of the rest.
- **Establish coverage**. We refer to those operations that consist of currencies other than the Euro, where a variation in the price can surely have a high financial cost.

Tips to Prepare for a Possible Financial Crisis

1- Free Yourself from Debts

In times of economic crisis, financial institutions often turn off the tap to grant credit as protection. It is one of its techniques for different clients who have debt capacity from those who do not.

Reaching a critical moment with a high level of debt is not beneficial at all, so it is advisable to pay them off as soon as possible and not take on more debt.

2- Choose the Right Time to Buy a Home

Acquiring a home is one of the most important decisions we make throughout our lives, specifically for the mortgage loan that will surely be associated with the purchase and will accompany us for at least two decades.

Waiting for the next stage of recession to happen to invest in real estate does not have to be a good decision because perhaps in the next crisis, prices will remain stable, and there will be no room for "bargains." It may also happen that prices drop, but mortgage interest rates soar.

When is the ideal time to buy a home then? The one in which we are able to face mortgage payments without our home economy suffering a great effort.

3- Promote Savings

As small as it may be, starting to create the habit of saving every month is essential to build a small mattress from which to survive in the event of an unexpected economic setback.

4- Plan for Your Retirement

In other countries like the US, creating an investment plan for when you reach retirement age is something that is integrated into your culture, and the profitability of pension plans grows steadily most of the time.

In our country, we are not so far-sighted, and the great variety of pension plans makes many of them unreliable, leading to ruin. The best advice? Be well advised on the product to be invested in.

The trends are divided. On the one hand, there are those who predict a new and close economic crisis; and on the other those who take iron out of the matter. The best advice in the face of uncertainty is to be forewarned.

5- Clean Up Your Treasury

For companies, having a healthy treasury with which to deal with unforeseen phenomena is increasingly important. Among the circles of financial experts, there has been a tendency to affirm that "Cash is king" or what is the same, having an excess of cash and liquidity is the best umbrella for when a storm is coming.

Chapter 8. Overcome Fear and Anxiety

Trading stocks is like playing a game of poker. You're competing against other traders, on the trading floor and in the virtual world. One of the most common fears traders face is a fear of losses. This can be because they are over-invested in one particular trade and don't want to lose any more money, or because they're afraid that their luck will run out. Either way, it's important that you recognize these fears and deal with them before they get the best of you. One way to get over a fear of losses is to simply accept that you will lose money. That's right—you will lose money. Everyone loses money. Some people lose a lot of money. But the only way to make money is to take risks, and sometimes those risks don't pay off. In fact, the more risk you take, the greater the potential for loss.

But that's also the reason why you can have such big profits when those risks pay off. So, if you can accept that you're going to lose money, then you won't be as scared when it happens. Another way to overcome this fear is to learn from your mistakes and move on. If you make a bad trade, don't try to convince yourself that you'll get in at the bottom and make it back. Sometimes, you will. Sometimes, you won't. And one of the ways you'll know whether you'll make it back is by looking at your last trade and seeing whether it was a mistake. Was it an accident? Was it a bad judgement call? Or was it a mistake in your analysis of the market? If it was the latter, then you can learn from that and move on to your next. If it was the former, you can just swallow your losses and move on.

Finally, if you have a hard time getting over the fear of losing money, try to view it as an opportunity. When you lose money, it's because you made a mistake. But that mistake is actually an opportunity for you to improve and get better. You can learn from that mistake and not make it again. You can find out what you did wrong and fix it so that the next time you trade, you'll be more confident. And you can be sure that the next time you trade, you'll do everything in your power not to make that mistake again. This way, when you lose money, it's not something to be afraid of. It's something to learn from and move on.

In summary, if you're afraid of losing money, keep in mind that it's a natural part of trading. You're going to lose money sometimes, and it's important that you are able to accept that. If you're making a mistake, don't convince yourself that you'll get your money back. Try to learn from what you did wrong so that it doesn't happen again. And if you view losing money as an opportunity to improve, it will be easier to deal with. I wish you the best of luck with your trading and hope that you can overcome your fear of losses.

Chapter 9. Some Simple Options Trading Strategies

Options trading features a wide variety of trading styles. They range from the basic, one-legged trades to the complex, multi-legged trades. The best part is that all strategies are based on two basic types. These are call options and put options. As a beginner, you should focus on learning one or two basic styles of trading. Once you master these styles adequately, you can then consider expanding your knowledge.

1. The Long Call

This strategy is very simple and pretty basic. It is ideal for beginners. Basically, as a trader, you find a call option and purchase it. This is known as going long. When you buy this option, you are doing so in the hope that the value of the underlying security will go up past the strike price within a given timeframe.

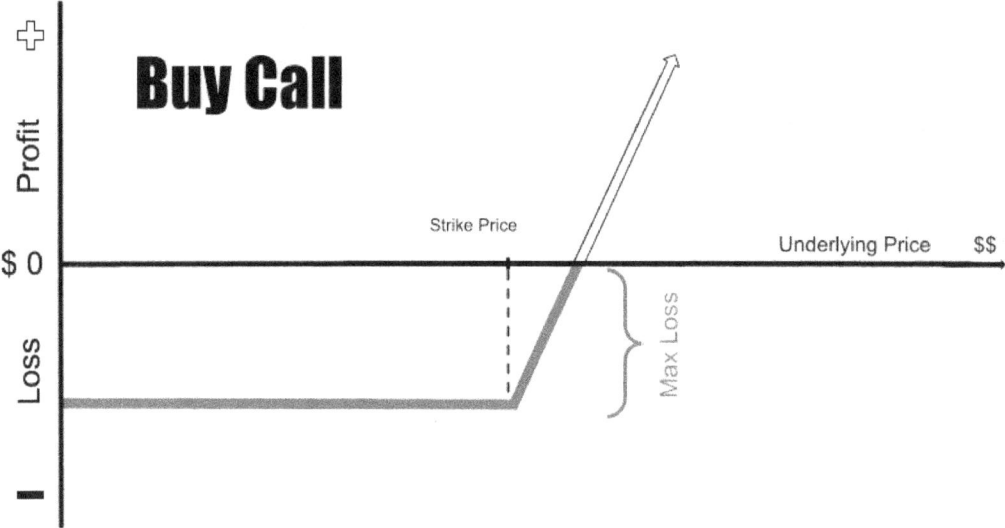

Example: Let us assume that a stock ABC is trading at $50. Let us also assume that a call option is available at $5 per share for a period of 6 months. Like all others, this option contract is for 100 shares. This means that it will cost you or any other trader $5 * 100 = $500 for the contract.

Possible Outcomes

Now if everything works out as planned, then the possibilities or chances of striking it big are limitless. All that you need to hope for is for the price to move upwards. If the stock price hits the $100 mark, then your possible earnings could top $4,500. The linear progression of this kind of trade is limitless. The worst that could happen is you could lose the premium you paid for the contract. In this instance, you could lose $500.

You should use this strategy if you think that the risk is worth the reward. In this case, the risk is pretty low and the rewards are potentially very impressive. It also saves you the hustle of actually buying the stock while still ensuring you benefit from them.

2. The Long Pull

Another very popular and very basic strategy is known as the Long Pull. This strategy is very similar to the long call. The only difference here is that you will be rooting for a price fall of the underlying stock. A drop-in price will put you in a better position to have the outcome that you desire.

Practical Example

Let us assume that ABC stock is at a price of $50. Now someone puts up a $50 put option. Each costs $5 and is limited in time to a 6-month period. So, if you were to buy a contract for 100 shares at $5 * 100 = $500. With this trade, you stand to benefit the most if the price drops to zero. Should this happen, then you will stand to make at least $5,000. On the other hand, the downside is that you will lose the premium you paid to acquire the stocks. In our case, this is $500.

Other Strategies

There are a number of other strategies that you can use. They include the covered call, the married put, and the short put. Here they are in brief:

The short put: This kind of trade is the direct opposite of the long put. Traders will sell their put or go short. The thinking or reasoning here is that the price of the stock will go up or remain stagnant until expiration.

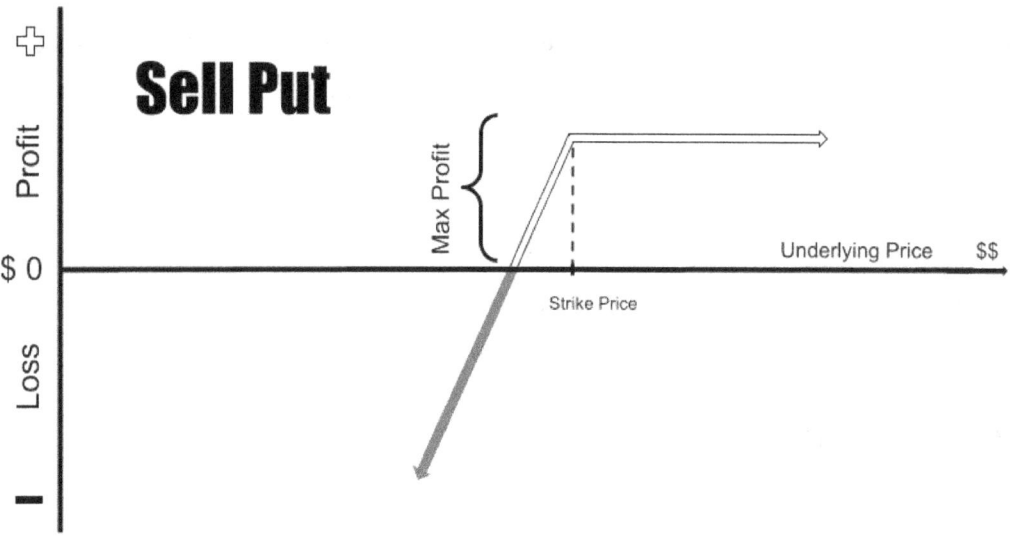

The payoff of a short put is the exact opposite of a long put.

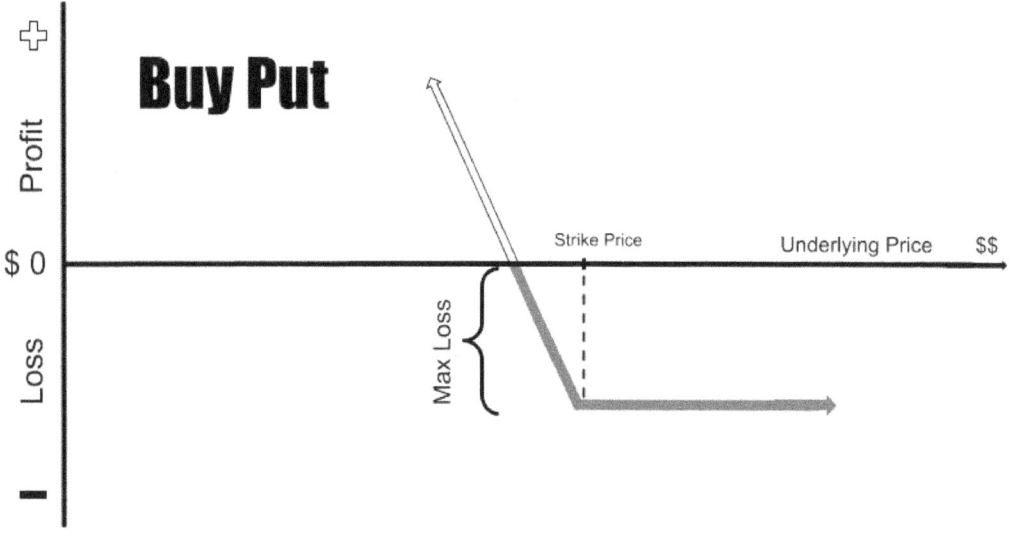

Chapter 10. Financial Leverage

For you to understand well the meaning of financial leverage, we will try to break down the terminology and explain it in a very simpler yet most understandable format as possible.

You will be able to define and understand why leverage may turn out to be riskier, the pros of using leverage in options trading and the level at which you need to use leverage in business for better returns.

Definition

Leverage comes from the word lever, which simply means a rod or bar that is used in science to aid in lifting loads. Actually, a lever makes work easier. Similarly, leverage is simply the advantage that is gained mechanically through the use of levers to lift loads.

It can be put diagrammatically as below:

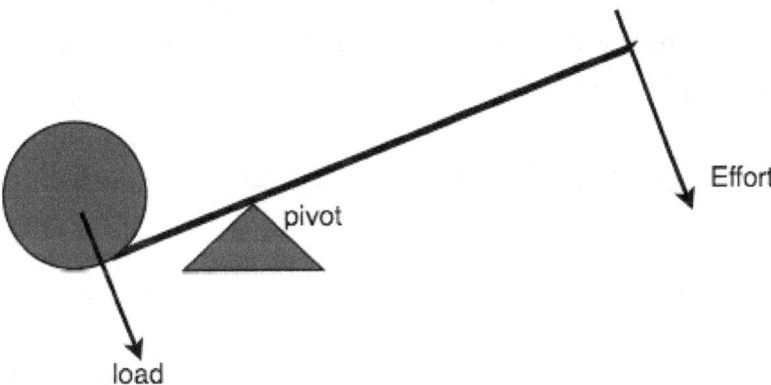

As you can see above, the lever is being used to lift the load as the effort is exerted on the load at point A over the pivot or the fulcrum. When the position of the pivot is altered, much effort is required to lift the load through the same distance.

In the same way, financially, leverage can be applied using the same logic and criteria—for example, the operations as well as financials. We will, therefore, have financial and operating leverage.

Therefore, leverage simply means the profit chances that prevail in the trade as a result of some basic inputs called costs. The nature of the costs is static.

This is the increased mechanism of achieving some objective; to increase the ability to apply standard-cost assets, in maximizing the profits for the investors.

When we talk about financial leverage, we simply refer to the association between what the company earns before taxes and other interests.

Why Leverage Is Referred to as a Risky Project

With leverage, it is like a businessman balancing on the coin. As you know, it is hard to balance on a coin because of its nature of instability. Leveraging in business is as technical and difficult to predict just like gambling. You cannot predict the outcome; however; such businesses are the most rewarding supposing you land on luck.

When the possibility of gaining more rewards goes high, there is a subsequent risk of initial investment and risk of getting equivalent losses. When dealing with brokerages, they will require that you keep your margin accounts to some standards.

Your securities and the cash will serve as collateral to everything you will have borrowed, that will tone down the broker's risk. This, in turn, increases your risk, suppose you over-borrow, and the position turns out to be a loss that means that you will have to lose whatever is on your account and as well be able to pay brokers' borrowed money.

How Leverage Is Used for the Benefit of the Trader

a. Trading Stocks

This means that for every market position, you need to invest a certain amount of money. You could be having a little amount, yet you need more in order to stand up for a given position. Therefore, you will be required to borrow some amount from the stockbrokers who give you money belonging to a certain stock.

Assume you lose the position at the end; it means that not only your money is lost, but that of the broker is also lost. You will be indebted to the broker still. Do you see how risky it could be at the end?

b. Trading Crypto

This sounds more different from the trading stock leverage. In this case, it is the lending market that is put to task. You will be allowed to borrow the currency that is crypto in nature, such as bitcoins, through your brokerage or rather goes in for the exchange.

Suppose you do not own any bitcoins, to begin with, the leverage trading will be very appealing. The coins are highly marketable because they go up in value unpredictably and without any prior warning. In this case, you need to be very alert else because you may end up losing a great deal.

Pros and Cons for Leverage Trading

Pros

a. More Capital with Less Hustle

You only require having a certain percentage of the total capital for a position, and the rest of the capital will be given to you by the brokerages.

b. Easy to Invest

The fact that you do not need to have enough money on your account makes it easy for many to invest using leverage than it would have been with stocks or other options in general.

c. No Initial Pain

The client or the investor does not need to lose much time and energy sourcing funds for the business. As long as you understand the procedures, rules, and regulations of the business, you are good to go.

d. Easy to Manage

What makes many people feel like losing the game of this business is the pain of looking for the capital and the subsequent hustle to ensure that you make profits. In this case, you are only required to monitor the trends and the way the shifting in the trends is affecting the market, rather than physically toiling to get profits like in stock markets.

Cons

a. It Is Unpredictable

It is not easy to tell when the net jackpot will be hit. The nature of the business is volatile, and therefore, it is not so easy to predict the outcome from the beginning. This makes the trader sick of anxiety for the time being until he hits the jackpot.

b. Permanent Loses

There is double loss in the case the deal flops. This is because, on top of your initial investment, you also went ahead to obtain credit from the brokers who would want their money repaid as soon as the expiry date or time elapses or as soon as the business ends.

If the contract closes on a loss, both your capital and the borrowed amount are lost. You have the obligation of paying the debt as well as nursing the loss of your initial investment.

Trading Smarter with Options

Trading smarter does not mean working hard to realize more profits. This involves the aspect of research in your market and business and working around the clock for the better of the business. You employ the readily and easily available tools and time to get the most out of them.

Advantages of Employing the Right Mindset

Work Out the Right Habits

For you to achieve much out of your trading game, you need to fine-tune your character and habits to suit the business. It becomes a big waste if you are not working up to the standards of the business because of the limitations within you. You need to embrace the good habits and for the unnecessary ones, say goodbye.

Use Time Wisely

In business, we say that time is money. The time you invest in business should be equivalent to the returns you get, otherwise time is wasted. You need to sophisticate your research procedures and trading strategies to cut off-screen time wastage.

Be Cool but Vigilant

Whenever there is a stress factor, you need to remain calm. Recollect your mind, assess the situation, and try to compare with other situations and allow yourself time to relax. Do you feel like panicking or stressed? Cool down and wait for the right moment for you to make decisions.

Decisions made in haste are usually negative in the trading program. So, ensure that every decision made results from a sober mind.

Risk Management in Option Trade

Just like any other financial investment, there are various risks involved in options trading. For most investments, it is always assumed that the higher the returns, the higher the risks involved. This is not the case with the options business. Here, the risk-reward ratio is significantly balanced since it is possible to make high returns from small investments. The risk involved in the trade is minimal compared to the reward.

When it comes to trading options, various techniques are used, and each of them has a certain level of risk. The good thing is that as a trader, you get to choose the level of risk you want to take. For each options contract that you sign and the orders you place, you can easily make a balance to lower the risks involved.

The more you learn about the trade, the more you will understand how easy it is to overcome most risks. Your success in the business partly depends on this. However, you must understand that whatever risk is involved in options is quite low as compared to the risk of trading your stock or underlying securities directly. The only common risk with options is losing your initial deposit, also known as the premium.

If you control your contracts with accuracy, you can always make a profit from the trade. For example, if you own 1,000 shares of a certain company and you think that the prices may go down in the future, you can get ten options and trade them at a profit instead of selling off your shares. This way, you will save your stock from declining market prices. Some long-term equity anticipation procedures allow you to do this for a period of up to two years.

Predefined Risks

The strategies used in options trading allow you to calculate the maximum risk involved in each contract. This is a great advantage to options traders because you are able to anticipate your profits or losses beforehand.

It gives you the confidence required in the trade since you would already have taken away the fear of the unknown. By spreading your trades and adjusting the size of your strikes, you will be able to minimize potential losses accordingly.

When starting up, setting up some risk management strategies can be difficult. As time goes by and you get familiar with the basics of trading, you will easily set up a combination of strategies to maximize every opportunity to make money.

By now, you have understood how options can limit your risks as you make unlimited profits. As a trader, you only have a right and not an obligation to engage in a trade. When the cost of an option is not good at expiration time, the buyer forfeits the right, in this case, the premium, allowing the contract to expire worthlessly.

Generally, options require less financial equity than other financial instruments. Although they are more dependable than stock, the level of risk involved depends on how you trade. If you are a careless trader, you will end up risking more, and losing a lot.

However, you can use the stop-loss order feature to prevent you from losing beyond a certain percentage of your premium. This order restricts the trade from going beyond the indicated limit and may save you from incurring big losses.

Let's say you purchase stock at $55 but do not want to lose more than 10% of this. You can place a $44 order to sell your option when the trade hits the $44 mark. Options are known for their high returns. When they pay off, the profits are good.

Avoid Leverage

As we all know that leveraging is borrowing shares from brokers to enable us to take up bigger positions hoping that in the future, we will gain more profits from these positions. Purchasing on-margin implies that you go in for a loan in order to fund your position. What you need is only a deposit for some shares, and then the rest is on loan. The problem comes in when the expectations are never met. You will be forced to return the borrowed money from your other savings.

Chapter 11. Money Management Concept

Money Concept in Option Trading

When working with options, it can provide you with some good leveraging power. A trader will be able to buy an option position that will imitate their stock position quite a bit, but it will end up saving them a lot of money in the process.

Let's say that you saw that there was an opportunity to make a profitable trade, you were only able to spare about $1000 to purchase the stock, but you didn't know what options were available. If we were still talking about the cows from before, you would not be able to purchase even one cow for the money (remember that they are about $2,000 each without the options contract), and so you would completely miss out on the possibility to make a profit.

But, if you decided to purchase with an options contract, rather than purchasing the underlying asset outright, the dynamics have completely changed. This could result in an investment of just $250 to get started. The premium on the options contract is a fraction of the total cost, allowing you to get in on the trade for a lot less money. If you look into options contracts, you will be able to make more purchases, and potentially more money, compared to some of the other stock choices you can make.

Exercise and Expiration

When there's a lot of time left for the options contract to expire, chances are high that the price of the underlying asset will undergo significant changes. Thus, the premium will be high. On the other hand, as the expiration approaches, the chances of significant change in the price of underlying assets tend to diminish, thus lowering the premium. The date of expiration causes options to have a definitive nature. Thus, if the price of an option seems unbearable, you might consider waiting for the expiration date to thin out.

Delivery and Settlement

Every contract for options will have a strike price associated with it. Of any of the given index or stock that is traded, there are going to be various options contracts that correspond with various strike prices. These prices are determined ahead of time by the stock exchange where the stock is traded.

Analysis of Costs and Benefits in the Options

The leveraging power of options is great. Thus, a trader may acquire an option position similar to a stock position, but at a significantly lower price. With options trading, it is possible to make great profits without necessarily having large amounts of money. Individuals that operate on a tight budget have found options trading very accommodating. A shrewd trader can employ leverage to increase their trading power without necessarily injecting more capital.

Let's suppose that you had $1000 and wanted to invest in a company whose stock was trading at $20 per share. On the one hand, you could choose to buy the company's stocks and thus acquire 50 shares. If the stock price increases to $25, you would make a $5 profit for every share you own, and your total profit would be $250. This is a 25% return on investment! On the other hand, you could purchase call options on the same stock and gain the right to purchase it. Assuming that the call options with a $20 strike price were trading at $2, you could purchase 500 options, which would enable you to purchase 500 shares. Assuming that the stock price increased to $25, you could exercise your option to purchase 500 shares and, upon selling your shares, you'd make a grand total of $2500. This is a staggering 150% return on investment! The greatest appeal of options trading is that it enables traders to execute cost-efficient trades even as it widens their earning capacity.

Risks Leverage

We rarely talk about how we can troubleshoot arising problems, or even reduce the degree of financial risks we must take in the first place. Though by no means extensive, I've included a short (but hopefully helpful) preview of the ways in which we can work on doing this with the first 48 hours of trading.

- **Trade with this approach in mind**: focus your attention and effort toward avoiding risks, rather than securing potential rewards. If you're not convinced, think about this little statistic recorded from a 2013 U.S Trust survey: 60% of millionaire investors place more emphasis on avoiding unnecessary risks than securing potential capital gain.
- **Diversify your account**. This is essentially just a fancy word for "split up your money to make it safer." When you don't put all of your eggs in one basket, so to speak, you significantly (and technically eliminate) the risk of losing all of your money when one investment opportunity cracks or crumbles.
- **Keep a broker or brokerage close by**. Beginner traders can benefit greatly from having a highly-trained, experienced financial expert or professional just a phone call or drive away. When trades don't go your way, or you're simply not deriving the benefits you expected

from trades, even within that initial 48-hour timeframe, a broker can assist and advise you on how to produce better results and generate more meaningful profit. Or they can attempt to remedy current, negative financial situations or trades.

Trading Rules You Should Know

The most common form of underlying assets that the majority of options contracts are based on are the shares of a publicly listed company. But an underlying asset can take other varied forms, such as the following:

- Index options: These have a close similarity to stock options, except that the index, not the shares, is what the options are based on.
- Forex/Currency options: The contracts of this nature give the owner the authority to purchase or sell off a certain currency at an agreed exchange rate.
- Futures options: The specified futures contract is the underlying security. A futures option allows the owner to enter into a specific futures contract.
- Basket options: The underlying asset can comprise a set of securities, such as currencies, stocks, commodities, and other financial securities.
- Commodity options: For this kind of contract, the underlying asset can be a commodity that is physical or based on futures contract.

Chapter 12. Analyzing Market Trends In Options Trading

Nearly every option trader has heard the old trade adage that says, "*The trend is your buddy.*" In reality, an option trading against the current market trend certainly puts the odds of winning for you. So many newcomers have lost whole accounts through the purchasing of call options from the bear trend market and the purchasing of options from the bull trend market.

So, what is a business phenomenon exactly?

Similarly, you know it's a bullish phenomenon when you see the bigger and higher indexes like the Dow Jones Industrial Average or the S&P500, and you realize it's a weird phenomenon when you see the smaller and lower indexes.

Yes, market patterns are general movements that tend to shift stocks. During a bull market, the prices of most stocks will rise and grow, and during the bear market the prices of most stocks will decline and drop.

One thing about trends is, however, that they are a "general course of movement." It does not mean that a bull trend just drives the market up every day and does not mean that a bear trend just drives the market down.

When you watch the ocean tides, the water does not rush on the beach in a rising tide, but falls in waves. One wave is stronger than the last. The same is true for stock market patterns. You will see days interspersed with days in a bull cycle. However, notifications will occur more regularly and after every slight retreat.

Traders who fall for either trap are usually shocked when the general trend resumes and are stuck in a losing position that never turns around.

Recognizing how patterns work is just the first step to business patterns identification. Have you ever believed that the economy is just one way for two people to disagree about it? How can two people who look at the same market draw different conclusions about the trend in the market?

The challenge of understanding consumer patterns is that the demand can be in all three directions at any point on the same day!

The market might be in a downturn for day traders, but on the same day, it could be in a bull downturn for a day trader and a long-term investor's neutral pattern. How can that be?

In reality, there are not just "business" conditions; depending on the timeframe, there are multiple market conditions! It is not known that there is a common consumer trend for various trade horizons and investment targets, which contributed to all the pointless debates about what the business trend is in television.

A diagram that looks incredibly strange in the 1-minute table might look extremely stable and chaotic on a regular map. As such, trend analysis includes in the first place an appreciation of the exact time frame in which you trade.

Acknowledgment of the exact time you are trading is an extremely important precondition for options trading, where the contracts and positions you have bought are time-sensitive! Yes, options don't last forever, and all choice approaches have an optimized return period.

For example, the market trend you would be concerned with will be the intraday trend most widely associated with minute charts, whether you are trading on the day with options and either writing or purchasing the options to close them for profit by the end of the trading day.

In this situation, whether the market is in a long-term bull or bear trend no longer affects your trading. The world may be crying, but if your minute charts show bearish for the day, the way you make your money is bearish.

If you trade a covered call, you will want to write the call options on a stock that is fairly lateral to the market trading charts in the regular charts if you want to prevent the allocation of stocks.

In comparison, if you buy long-term LEAPS options, you may be more interested in what the long-term market trend is, instead of being too concerned with uncertainty every day.

So, what are the most important methods for identifying business trends?

Most veterans can identify the pattern in which a map looks much like a price chart. However, countless complex technological metrics have been developed over the years for the less skilled or technically-inclined.

Personally, the Simple Moving Average is the most tested. It simply averages the price over a period of time to see where it normally goes. This is what I focus on most of the time personally and I use a different average period for different time horizons. The 30days or 50days are most widely used.

Chapter 13. Recognizing Trading Opportunities

A key piece of options trading centers on discovering chances to make exchanges. There are various ways that you can recognize and survey such chances, and we have given data on what is engaged with the procedure. To be effective in your exchanging, you will have a lot of chances for trades, so this is unquestionably something you should give an opportunity to.

On the off chance that you have been perusing this guide so as to assist you with beginning with options trading, you will thoroughly understand the underlying readiness required and how to pick a trader. You'll additionally have a comprehension of exchanging levels and how they can influence your capacity to utilize certain procedures.

At this stage, it's an ideal opportunity to begin pondering how you are going to discover chances to exchange. You could know totally everything there is to think about options trading, however, such information is just valuable in the event that you can really try everything and recognize chances to make a few profits.

Despite the fact that options trading is actually very perplexing, anybody that is set up to invest energy learning the subject can eventually be effective. Be that as it may, realizing how to trade options isn't enough without nothing else; you have to realize how to bring in the money out of it. This takes difficult work and responsibility; you should invest the necessary effort so as to locate the correct options and afterward make the proper exchanges.

In the event that you can do that reliably, at that point you will very likely accomplish your objectives. On this page, we take a look at how you approach distinguishing possibly beneficial open doors for trading options.

1. Which Underlying Assets?

Despite the fact that options contracts are resources themselves, they are really subordinating in that get their incentive from the hidden resources which they identify with. Options contracts can be purchased and sold on a wide scope of basic resources that incorporate stocks, remote monetary forms, wares, and lists.

This makes options trading a truly adaptable type of contributing in light of the fact that, you can make speculations on a wide range of monetary instruments just by purchasing and selling options contracts.

This implies one of the principal things you have to consider whenever you are searching for potential options trading openings is actually which of these money-related instruments you need to incorporate.

It ought to be evident that you don't have to choose to exchange just investment opportunities, or just forex options, or just wallet options. You can purchase and sell the same number of various sorts of choices as you feel great with. Be that as it may, you do need to consider how you will be examining potential exchanges and how you'll be recognizing appropriate chances.

On the off chance that you concluded that you would think about a wide range of various hidden securities, at that point you would be giving yourself the most obvious opportunity with regard to discovering openings due to the wide scope of conceivable outcomes. You should be ready, however, to complete a great deal of investigation into various money-related markets, which could be very tedious and it could really make it exceptionally hard to locate the number of chances you might want.

On the other hand, on the off chance that you concluded that you were just going to exchange stock options dependent on stocks in a specific division, at that point you would have the option to concentrate your examination explicitly on publically recorded organizations that work around it. You may wind up turning into a specialist in that field and be significantly more adroit at distinguishing related open doors dependent on this skill.

The drawback, obviously, to adopting such a restricted strategy is that you might be passing up lots of different open doors in various segments and markets that you aren't in any event, taking a look at.

There truly is no correct way, or incorrect way, to move toward this part of distinguishing openings and we wouldn't offer particular guidance in such a manner. All we would recommend is that you set aside the effort to consider which fundamental resources you need to incorporate and afterward it's eventually down to what you feel great with and what you think will give you the most obvious opportunity with regard to progress.

On the off chance that you do have solid information about a specific segment or market, at that point it would bode well to use that information; however, there is likewise nothing wrong with taking a more extensive view either. You may conclude that you would prefer not to inquire about and investigate the fundamental resources of options, yet would prefer to contemplate the value of the developments of the options contracts themselves and exchange in a similar manner.

2. Doing Research

The coming of the plan and online innovation has influenced exchanging and interest in more than one way. Not just has it brought about online dealers, which make the entire procedure of purchasing and selling of monetary instruments a lot simpler, it has additionally made data identifying with money-related instruments significantly more open.

The web provides limitless information that can be used for all intentions and purposes, and this truly is significant to financial specialists. It's fundamental to begin checking the trades to get modern statements and to follow universal news that can influence the business sectors. In any event, getting money-related reports on publically recorded organizations is something essential to do. The web is a rich wellspring of realities, measurements, and figures that can help gigantically.

Obviously, gathering data is just a single piece of doing research for exchanging purposes. The genuine aptitude is in comprehending what data to search for and afterward realizing how to decipher it. This is an ability in itself, yet it's an expertise that can be effortlessly evolved after some time with a lot of training.

In the event that you are set up to invest a considerable measure of time to researching and breaking down what you discover, then you truly will give yourself a greatly improved possibility of progress with regard to finding conceivably beneficial chances.

3. Central and Technical Analysis

Central investigation and specialized examination are the two main strategies utilized by speculators and brokers to break down data and help figure out what exchanges and projects to make. In spite of the fact that they are both basically utilized for a similar reason, they are altogether different in the manner in which they are utilized.

Essential examination is fundamentally about gathering however much data as could reasonably be expected, identifying with a particular security and afterward dissecting that data to decide the genuine estimation of that security and how it identifies with its exchanging cost.

For instance, on the off chance that you need to do central investigation on a stock in a specific organization, at that point you would consider various parts of that organization, for example, their current money-related quality, their profit reports, the nature of their administration workforce, and their serious edge in the commercial center. By doing this, you could get a thought of whether the stock was underestimated, exaggerated, or estimated directly comparable to its actual worth. This is to some degree improved, yet it gives you a thought of how essential investigation is utilized.

Specialized investigation is based on utilizing past information to foresee future developments. It includes considering and dissecting outlines and diagrams delineating cost and volume, with the end goal of discovering designs that could uncover patterns that are probably going to be rehashed. The hypothesis is that by following those patterns you can make precise estimates about how a security is going to move in cost over a given period of time. Once more, this is a genuinely streamlined perspective on specialized examination, yet it's a sensible outline of what is included.

Both basic examination and specialized investigation are commonly utilized by speculators in stocks; however, they have their use in options trading as well. The general thought is that you would utilize these strategies to assist you with getting a thought of how you would anticipate that the cost of money-related instruments should move, and afterward exchange the fitting options contracts to profit by those moves.

Neither central investigation nor specialized examination can truly be viewed as better than the other one as there are various variables to consider. It rather boils down to individual inclination; in the event that you feel increasingly good utilizing one of the procedures for your examination, or have a specific fitness for it, at that point it clearly bodes well to utilize that strategy. You may like to utilize a mix of both or utilize central investigation in certain conditions and specialized examination in others.

It merits noting, however, that options trading is frequently about exploiting transient value developments as opposed to whatever else. Crucial examination can assist you with increasing comprehension of the innate worth of a security, and it is usually utilized by long-haul financial specialists to put resources into underestimated stocks that ought to go up in cost after some time. Be that as it may, it doesn't really assist you with foreseeing value developments in the prompt term.

Specialized examination can, which is the reason options dealers are most likely bound to profit by utilizing specialized investigation: especially those utilizing a day exchanging style and making a few short exchanges regularly.

Something else to consider when you are recognizing potential exchanges is how much capital is required and how much hazard is included. Dealing with your spending plan and your introduction to hazard is a significant piece of options trading.

Hazard and Money Management

Great administration of your introduction to chance and your exchanging capital is totally crucial in any type of exchanging on the off chance that you can bring in the money over the long haul. There are various techniques you can use for overseeing risks and controlling your spending plan, for example, utilizing options spreads and position estimating; our article on risk and cash the board covers a few of the best ones. We additionally offer guidance on the most proficient method to utilize them.

Effectively dealing with your capital and risk introduction is basic when trading options. While chance is basically unavoidable with any type of project, your introduction to chance doesn't need to be an issue. The key is to deal with the risk reserves viably; consistently guarantee that you are okay with the degree of risk being taken and that you aren't presenting yourself to unreasonable losses.

Chapter 14. The Greeks

Delta

The concept behind delta is actually pretty straightforward and easy to apply. It tells you how much the price of an option is going to change if the price of the underlying stock changes by one dollar. Consider a delta of 0.68. If the underlying stock changes by one dollar, that tells us that the price of the option will change by $0.68.

The way the Delta changes with time depends on a few factors. Let's take an in-the-money call option first. When it is in the money, delta increases with the passage of time. The reason why this happens is that extrinsic value is decreasing, while intrinsic value remains directly proportional to the price of the stock. Therefore, delta will increase. At first, this effect is barely noticeable if at all. The less time remaining for the option, the more noticeable it will be.

Now let's consider a call option that is out of the money. In that case, Delta will decrease.

For comparison suppose that we have a call option with a strike price equal to $100. Suppose further that there are 10 days left to expiration. If the underlying stock price is $99 (so that the call option is out of the money) delta is 0.43. On the other hand, if the share price was $101, (so that the option was in the money), delta would be 0.59.

This demonstrates that when the option goes in the money, with all else being equal, it is more heavily influenced by the price of the underlying shares.

Under the conditions specified with the price of the stock at $101, the price of the call option is $2.54. Suppose that the price of the stock goes up to $102. Since Delta is 0.59, we expect the $1 rise in share price to raise the price of the option by $0.59, to $3.13.

It raises it a little more, to $3.16, so it was a pretty good estimate. As the price changes delta changes as well. In this case, it jumped to 0.66, meaning that an additional rise in price by $1 will have a greater impact.

Of course, that cuts both ways; delta gives us an estimate of how much the price of the option will drop as well. If we have a value of delta equal to 0.66, we expect a $2 drop in share price to lead to a drop in the price of the option by $1.32. What actually happens is that the price of the call drops down to $1.98, not quite as much as expected. A declining share price means a declining delta, and in this example, it drops to 0.51. This implies that the next dollar that the share price drops will have less impact.

When options are at the money, delta will be close to 0.50 in all cases.

For call options, delta is a positive value. It ranges from zero all the way to up to 1.0. The more that the option goes in the money, the higher that Delta will be.

Let's consider our share price at a hundred dollars and suppose instead that we were looking at an option with a strike price of $90. In that case, delta is a very strong 0.98. Therefore, we would expect the price of the option to rise by nearly $1 for every $1 rise in share price. The price of this option under these conditions will be $10.04. Now, if we increase the share price by $1, we find that the price of the option will increase to $11.02. So, the correspondence between the actual change in option price and delta gets stronger, the more "in the money" the option is. Continuing our current example, a strike price of $85 would give us a call option with a delta of exactly 1.0.

If an option is out of money, the closer it gets to expiration the smaller delta gets. In fact, it will quickly go to zero.

Now let's have a look at put options.

For put options, delta is given as a negative value. So, the range for a put option is from zero to -1.0. The meaning is basically the same. It is a negative value because, in the case of put options, price movements of puts move in the opposite direction to stock value. In other words, put options become more valuable as stock prices drop.

The negative sign indicates that a drop in the price of a share of stock by a dollar is going to cause a rise in the option price—when we are talking about put options.

This means that changes in share price are going to be a little more influential for the option. If a put option is strongly in the money, delta will approach -1.0. Remember that, as the expiration date approaches for a call option, delta goes to zero if the option is out of the money. Put options exhibit the same behavior.

Delta can also be thought of in different ways. For example, it can estimate the probability that an option will expire in the money. So, let's say that you have a call option with the Delta of 0.7. That tells you that there is a 70% chance that the option will expire in the money. Another call option, that had a delta of 0.5, only has a 50% chance of expiring in the money. But remember that delta is dynamic, so that value is only the probability at this very moment. A significant change in stock price might change the situation, and one more business day will also impact it.

Gamma

Now, let's have a look at the next Greek, which is Gamma. This one is a little bit more obscure. Gamma can be thought of as the second derivative if you have experience with calculus. If you have no experience with calculus or you want to forget it, I apologize for the headache.

Basically, what that means is that Gamma gives the rate at which delta will change if there is a one-dollar change in the underlying stock price. As a side note, if you do remember from calculus, a derivative of position with time is speed or velocity. So, you can think of Delta as giving the speed or velocity in the change of price of the option.

Gamma, in this analogy, would be the acceleration in the change of the option price. Understanding the details and all the mathematics is not important for most options traders. However, you can keep some basic rules of thumb in mind. The key point is this. The higher gamma is the more responsive to changes the option is going to be in the underlying stock price.

Another way to think of this is to know that Delta changes every time the underlying stock price changes. So, Delta is only as good as the value that we see at a given instance. You can use Gamma to estimate how Delta will change when there is price movement. The further you are from expiration, the higher the Gamma will be.

The more an option goes in the money, the smaller Gamma will get. What that means is that Delta won't be changing as much for a given change in the price of the underlying stock if the option is in the money. If Delta goes to 1.0, then Gamma will go to zero.

Theta

It is a fact that the extrinsic value of an option is going to decrease as time passes. There is simply no way around this. When an option is further away from the expiration date, there are more opportunities for the stock price to fluctuate. This means that fluctuations in the stock price over a longer period of time could put an option that is currently out of the money, in the money. As you get closer to expiration, there are simply fewer opportunities for that to happen. So, an out-of-the-money option is not going to have as much value as days pass.

If you just play around with options prices using a calculator or watch them on the markets, it might seem a little bit mysterious how the extrinsic value changes. But you can use Theta to get an idea of what is happening. Theta gives an estimate of how much the price of the option will decrease each passing day. Specifically, it tells you how much the extrinsic or time value of the option will decrease.

Since Theta is telling you how much the extrinsic value is going to decrease, it is listed as a negative number. Consider an option with a $50 strike price and a share price of $53. At 15 days to expiration, Theta is -0.027 for a call option, and -0.026 for a put option. Let's look at the call option; the principle is about the same for both. This tells us that the extrinsic value at 14 days will drop by about $0.03. At 15 days to expiration, the extrinsic value is $0.29 for the call option. So, we are going to expect it to drop to $0.26 the following day. As a matter of fact, this is exactly what happens.

Time decay is exponential and not linear. If an option is in the money, Theta will decrease in value as the expiration date approaches. If it is out of the money, then it will increase. This indicates that an out-of-the-money option is going to lose value faster, the closer you get the expiration date.

An in-the-money option will smoothly lose extrinsic value as the expiration date approaches. At-the-money options will gain in value as the expiration date approaches. For at-the-money options, extrinsic value represents a higher proportion of their price as compared to other options. Even though Theta will be smaller for out-of-the-money options, it still represents a greater percentage of losses in price, because extrinsic value represents 100% of the total worth.

In any case, options always lose extrinsic value as the expiration date approaches.

Chapter 15. How Options Work

Options operators must understand the complexity that surrounds them. The knowledge of the operation of the options allows operators to make the right decisions and offers them more options when executing a transaction.

Indicators:

- The value of an option consists of several elements that go hand in hand with the "Greeks"
- The price of the guaranteed value
- Expiration
- Implied volatility
- The actual exercise prices
- Dividends
- Interest rates

The "Greeks" provide valuable information on risk management and help rebalance the portfolios to achieve the desired exposure (e.g., delta coverage). Each Greek measures the reaction of the portfolios to small changes in an underlying factor, which allows the individual risks to be examined:

- The delta measures the rate of change of the value of an option regarding changes in the price of the underlying asset.
- The gamma measures the rate of change in the delta concerning the changes suffered by the price of the underlying asset.
- Lambda or elasticity refers to the percentage change in the value of an option compared to the percentage change in the price of the underlying asset, which offers a method of calculating leverage, also known as "indebtedness."
- Theta calculates the sensitivity of the option value over time, a factor known as "temporary wear."
- Vega measures the susceptibility of the option of volatility. Vega measures the value of the option based on the volatility of the underlying asset.
- Rho represents the sensitivity of the value of an option against variations in the interest rate and measures the value of the option based on the risk-free interest rate.

Therefore, the Greeks are reasonably simple to determine if the Black-Scholes model (considered the standard option valuation model) is used and is very useful for intraday and derivatives traders. Delta,

Theta, and Vega are useful tools to measure time, price, and volatility. The value of the option is directly affected by maturity and volatility if:

• For a long period before expiration, the value of the purchase and sale option tends to rise. The opposite situation would occur if, for a short period before expiration, the value of the purchase and sale options is prone to a fall.

• If the volatility increases, so will the value of the purchase and sale options, while if the volatility decreases, the value of the purchase and sale options decreases.

• The price of the guaranteed value causes a different effect on the value of the purchase options than on that of the sale options.

• Usually, as the price of the securities increases, so do the current purchase options that correspond to it, increasing its value while the sale options lose value.

• If the price of the value falls, the opposite happens, and the current purchase options usually experience a drop in the value while the value of the sale options increases.

A Bonus of Options

It happens when an operator acquires an options contract and pays an initial amount to the seller. The options premium will vary depending on when it was calculated and on which market options its acquisition was made.

What Is the Value of the Contract Over Time?

Once an options contract expires, it loses its value. Therefore, it is logical that the longer the validity period, the higher the premium. This is because the deal has additional temporary costs and that more time is available in which the option can be profitable.

What level of volatility does the market have? The premium will be higher if the options market is more volatile as it increases the possibility of obtaining a more significant benefit from the option. The opposite principle applies to the lower volatility that implies a lower premium as the market is considered relatively "stable." The volatility of the options market is determined by using different price scales (the long-term, recent, and expected price scales are the required data) to a selection of price volatility models.

The sale and purchase options do not have equivalent values when they reach their mutual ITM, ATM, and OTM exercise price due to the direct and opposite effects caused by their oscillation in irregular distribution curves, which unbalances them.

Exercises—the number of exercises and increments between the exercises are decided based on the change that is applied to the product.

Option Valuation Models

It is essential to know the differences between historical and implicit volatility when applied for stock market purposes.

Historical volatility calculates the movement rate of the underlying asset in a given time in which the standard annual deviation of price changes is given as a percentage. Historical volatility is the retrospective measurement at the date of calculation of the information available on the degree of instability of the underlying asset in a given number of trading days (modifiable period) and during a selected period.

The implied volatility is the future approximation of the stock exchange volume of the underlying asset that measures the expected variation in the standard daily deviation of the asset between the date on which it is calculated and the maturity of the option. When analyzing the value of an option, implied volatility is one of the critical factors that an operator has to consider. To calculate implied volatility, an option valuation model is used, taking into account the cost of the option premium.

There are three types of theoretical valuation models that intraday traders use most frequently as an aid to assess implied volatility. These models are the Black-Scholes, the Bjerksund-Stensland, and the Binomial. With them, the calculation is done using algorithms, usually buy and sell options are used at-the-money or nearest-the-money.

The Black-Scholes model is the most used with European options (these options may only be executed on the day of expiration).

The Bjerksund-Stensland model is very efficient if applied to US options that can be executed at any time between the acquisition of the contract and its expiration.

The Binomial model is appropriately applied to American, European, and Bermuda options. Bermudas are a midpoint between European and American companies and can be executed only on certain days of the contract or on the expiration date.

Types of Options

There are two main kinds of options:

1. Selling Options

A given option is an option contract wherein the owner can, but is not required to, sell a specified amount of the underlying security at a given price within a certain period. This is the opposite of a purchase option. It gives the holder the right to purchase shares.

A sale option becomes more valuable as the price of the underlying share depreciates relative to the exercise price. On the contrary, a sale option loses its value as the underlying share appreciates and its maturity approaches.

The value of a sale option decreases with time since the chances of the stock falling below the specified strike price are less and less with time.

2. The Purchase Options

A call option is an agreement that gives the investor the right to buy stocks, bonds, commodities, or other instruments at a specified price within a specified period, but not the obligation.

The purchase option gives you the right to purchase an asset. When the underlying asset increases in price, you get benefits with a buy option. For example, if your share is priced at $50 and you buy your purchase option at $50, then you have the right to buy that share at $50, regardless of its price, as long as the time has not expired. Even if the stock goes up to $100, you still have the right to buy that stock for $50.

The Underlying Asset

Traditionally, most options have been based on shares of publicly traded companies. However, options based on other underlying investments are increasingly common. This includes options based on stock indices, traded funds (ETF), REIT (real estate investment funds), foreign exchange, and raw materials such as agricultural or industrial products. When it comes to stock options contracts, it is essential to keep in mind that they are based on 100 shares of the underlying value.

An exception would be when there are adjustments by the division of shares or mergers. It is also important to remember that the purchase of stock options is entirely different from the purchase of shares.

Chapter 16. Avoiding Beginner Mistakes and Tips

It's very easy for beginners to make mistakes when trading because it's exciting and stressful all at the same time. Let's take a look at some of the mistakes beginners are prone to, and think about how to avoid them.

Panicking and exiting early

I did emphasize that you should have a criterion for exiting a position that isn't going in your direction. However, you need to have some flexibility because small moves in the stock translate into big moves in an option. So, you might see your option show up at some $40 in the red. That is an unpleasant prospect but that means that the stock might have dropped by something like $.60.

Now, if you think about that, you know that it's not uncommon at all for a stock to drop $0.60 or $0.70, and then rebound in the upper direction by a dollar. So, to sell off your option just because there is a small dip like that—unless it's clear that it's part of the downward trend—would be a foolish move. But we can forgive beginners for making a mistake of that nature. It's easy to get panicky when you start seeing your money slip away right before your own eyes.

To deal with these types of situations it's really important to understand a little bit about technical analysis and candlestick charts. These topics are beyond the scope of this book, but you can find information about these topics online, on YouTube, and of course in many books. The point of learning these tools is so that you can look at the chart and estimate where the stock is heading. The tools are far from perfect, otherwise everyone would be multimillionaires.

However, they are pretty good at giving you an idea that I would call an educated guess. It's better to make an educated guess than it is to panic and sell your options. When I first started, I made the mistake of exiting positions far too early and I would look back later and find that if I had stayed in, I would've made a massive profit. Remember the stock market is always fluctuating a great deal.

Getting Involved in Many Trades at Once

As we've said multiple times spreading yourself too thin is a really bad idea when it comes to trading. No matter what strategy you decide to adopt, my belief is that you should focus on a few different securities and no more. So, what you might sit down and do is pick five stocks that you were really interested in. Hopefully, these are big companies because you want liquidity in the options.

Another thing you want is a relatively high share price so that the options have a chance to profit. Know if you are selling options or credit spreads, you definitely want a high share price so that you can earn from the premium.

Once you pick out your five companies, you should study everything about the companies and know them inside and out. That means looking at their financial statements, knowing when their earnings calls are, and keeping track of things like the volatility, and price-earnings ratio. Then you should study the charts of that company for the past 12 months. Familiarize yourself with the range that the price has gone through over the past year. None of this is foolproof but you were going to be far better off if you were informed rather than simply winging it when trading options.

So, what happens if you do more than five companies? At some point, you're going to be spreading yourself too thin. If you trade more than five at once it's going to be hard to keep track of the changes in the share prices of companies that you are trading. And to decide whether to get in or out of trades you need to be keeping a close eye on everything. Now, some people are maniacs and they are able to divide their attention very well and they like high pressure. If you are a so-called type of personality that likes high pressure, then maybe you can go with as many as you want. But my advice for beginners is that you were going to be better off focusing on a smaller number of companies that you can really study and pay attention to.

Using Too Many Strategies

As I said before, one of the first things you should do is to sit down and figure out what your goal is with trading options. You don't want to be using a haphazard approach and trying to do this and that and seeing what happens. Instead, decide what your goal is and the best way you want to achieve it in. Then look at all the different strategies that are available and see what is the most compatible with your goals. Then, apply maybe two or three different strategies at a time. There has to be some flexibility because some situations are going to require one strategy while other situations require a different strategy.

Taking Too Much Risk

If you noticed, with the strategies that we examined, there are some trade-offs that have to be made. The trade-offs often involve a trade-off between the amount of profit you can make and the level of risk. People are always greedy, I can guarantee that, but one thing that really does is to get you into trouble when it comes to trading. You need to be disciplined and methodical so that it means not taking

64

too much risk when it can be avoided. It's better to seek small profits in small bites that can add up rather than trying to hit a home run.

Set It and Forget It

This is a huge mistake the beginners make. They think buying an option is a cool idea, and so they buy an option. But then they don't spend every day studying it and following it. Maybe they hear on the news that the stock drop by five dollars. Then if they go to check their option, they might find that it lost $65 in value. Don't ever take a set-and-forget approach. Every option that you trade, you need to pay attention to in detail every day.

Forgetting About Time Decay

Time decay is one of the most important properties of options. Every day an option is losing extrinsic or time value. But some people leave their options for a long time hoping that the stock is going to move in a favorable direction. Then it never does and they end up losing money when the option expires worthless. So, you have to keep in mind that an option has time decay and that the option is going to lose value because of this. If it's not in the money, that means it's losing value overall.

When Selling Options, Stop Looking at Probabilities

One thing that can also be tempting is to always aim for the highest premium that you can earn when selling a credit spread. That is a bad strategy. Even though you might get a large credit, you might also put yourself at a high risk of assignment. The goal should be to set up trades that have a high probability of success. Would you rather have a trade that might make $200 but it has a 65% chance of failure, or would you rather have a trade that made $75 and had a 95% chance of success? I think it's the latter that would appeal to most people. The thing is the $75 is just one trade. You can do 10 or 20 of those trades.

Not Paying Attention to Volatility

Every time you look up an option, I advise you to look at the implied volatility. This is actually an estimate of the future volatility of the stock that underlies the option. If the implied volatility is high, that means higher option prices, generally speaking. If you're selling options, you are going to want to sell options where the implied volatility is higher. That is something that a lot of people ignore, once again beginners seem to only focus on the price they receive for the option.

Not Having a Training Plan

Besides setting general goals, you should have a trading plan in place. The first part of your training plan would be to establish how much money you're willing to risk on every trade. Another thing to look at is what strategy you're going to use to determine which trades to enter. For example, you might just do it on a whim when it seems like the stock is going up. In fact, that's how most people view the markets, but you could take a different approach. Instead of doing that, what you could do is having a technical analysis-based reason to enter a trade. For example, if the stock price has been dropping, but there's a golden cross, that means that a short-period moving average has crossed over on top of the lawn.

Moving average is a good sign that you should enter a trade. So, you could start your week picking out the stocks that you're interested in for that week. I advise working with a small number of stocks at any given time, so you could pick three such as Facebook, Lucky Martin, and Amazon. Then what you do is you study the charts and wait for the right moment to enter the trade.

Not Giving Enough Time or Even Thinking about Time

It's important to think about the expiration date that you pick when trading options. This needs to be taken into account when you watch the price of the auction going up and down. There is always a possibility that an option that it's going down is going to rebound later on if there is a long time until the expiration.

So, if there was only three days left for an option—and it was losing money— that is a trade that I would definitely say to cut your losses. But if there are three weeks left, panicking every time the option goes down in value is a really bad idea. Instead, you need to let it sit there and wait until the right moment to sell it. Even if that means only going so far is breaking even so, you can get out of the trade without losing money. But the time left to expiration is a very important factor in deciding how to handle that situation.

Chapter 17. Daily Routine for a Trader

Missteps occur in options trading. They regularly happen on the grounds that an excessive amount of data is coming in without a moment's delay and you feel over-burden, frozen, and forceful, or they frequently happen during calm/peaceful times when your watchman is down. Furthermore, obviously, there are constantly irregular mix-ups, for example, hitting an inappropriate catch—purchase rather than sell—or putting out an inappropriate position size. Such blunders can even occur with robotized methodologies.

Before each trading day, take a couple of minutes to practice multiple day trading routines to help limit mistakes for the duration of the day. Here are the means to practice. Depending on the market you exchange, you may wish to include a couple of extra advances. This entire procedure just takes a few minutes, however, spares you a great deal of dissatisfaction and cash.

1. Conditions in the Market

Make a brisk appraisal of trading conditions up until now. Is the pre-advertise demonstrating a great deal of instability, or is it steady? Is there a pattern or explicit propensities you notice?

Such an evaluation tells you how to continue, and whether you ought to exchange your framework by any stretch of the imagination. This is particularly significant if utilizing an emotional framework—a framework that fluctuates marginally dependent on economic situations. For instance, in unpredictable conditions, you may have a bigger expected benefit focus than on many days when there is no unpredictability.

2. Keep Notes

On your graph, put content notes expressing when high effect news discharges are. Whenever fascinated in an exchange, you may disregard one of these occasions, and it could cost you beyond all doubt. Record it on your diagram. In the event that the occasion happens later in the day, look over and put the content note close to the estimated time of the declaration. That way you will see it when the opportunity arrives.

3. Launch Platform is Vital

Dispatch your stage. Ensure statements are flowing (not slacking or sporadic) and the program is running easily. Most intermediaries give dependable and encouraging information, yet issues can emerge.

In the event that the information feed is irregular or appears to be erroneous, don't exchange until the issue is fixed. On the off chance that it looks right, continue.

4. Automated Strategies Should Be Confirmed

Regardless of whether you day exchange physically, you may have some robotized orders. For instance, in Ninja Trader and Meta Trader, you can convey stop loss requests and focuses on the minute you enter a position. Ensure these stop loss requests and targets are set properly. In the event that trading with a "robot," ensure all settings are exact before beginning it.

5. Have an End Time

In the event that you see a time you pattern to give back profits all the time, make a note to yourself to quit trading around then. Many informal investors will in general lose money in the time around (and including) the New York lunch hour if trading U.S. markets. In the event that you see this inclination, don't battle it. Quit trading during moments of the day you commonly lose money. Help yourself to remember this when you start trading every day.

6. Have a Starting Position Size

In the event that you exchange with a default position size, ensure it is set fittingly. Adding an additional digit to a position size could spell catastrophe. Dropping a digit implies you exchange a small amount of what you could have, and you pass up a chance.

On the off chance that you physically change your position size dependent on your entrance point and stop loss areas, note your record balance before trading. Legitimate position measuring limits risk to a little level of record capital, for example, 2%. In the event that you have a $40,000 account, you can risk up to $400 on an exchange. Remember this greatest risk for the duration of the day (or make a content note on your screen) to remind yourself this is the most you can risk on one exchange.

7. The Economic Calendar Must Be Considered

High impact monetary times can cause value spikes/holes, making critical slippage (the distinction between the value you expect and the value you get) on stop loss orders. It's ideal to abstain from being in exchanges for a couple of minutes around high impact news times. Check your monetary schedule before trading, and note the high impact news times. For U.S. stocks and prospects, you can utilize Bloomberg. For Forex, look at the Daily FX financial schedule.

On the off chance that you exchange individual stocks all the time, check the organization does not have income or different declarations due out that day. The Yahoo! Finance profit schedule functions admirably. Know about these occasions, to abstain from trading directly before the declaration.

8. Important Thoughts

Help yourself to remember your risky propensities, and how you will deal with those circumstances should they emerge. Go over your Key Trading Thoughts.

9. Be Mindful as You Start Trading

You are set to exchange. This procedure should help dispense with certain errors identified with position size, trading an inappropriate record/contract, trading during news or just not setting up your brain to exchange.

As you begin searching for potential exchange arrangements, remember your Key Trading Thoughts. This will help to keep you out of awful exchanges (ones not in your trading plan) and keep you warned and prepared to jump on great chances.

10. Use the Right Trading Account

In Meta Trader and Ninja Trader (for instance) you can sign in to various records utilizing a similar stage. Ensure you are trading the right record. Be particularly cautious on the off chance that you practice day trading in a mimicked record, yet additionally have live records. You would prefer not to have an incredible day, just to acknowledge you traded in recreation rather than with genuine capital. In the event that day trading prospects, ensure you are trading the rightmost noteworthy volume contract. Know about termination dates on the agreements you exchange.

11. Make a Trading Routine

Your day trading routine may shift marginally from this, contingent upon your trading style and the market you exchange. Make a daily schedule, however. It just takes about a moment or two to practice, and can spare you from a great deal of dissatisfaction.

Chapter 18. Selling Naked Options

What's a Naked Option?

A naked choice, likewise referred to as an "uncovered" option, is produced once the seller of an option agreement doesn't use the main security required to satisfy the possible obligation which results from the offering (also referred to as "writing" or maybe "shorting") of an option. Offering a function generates an obligation of the seller to present an option customer with the basic shares or maybe futures contract for any corresponding lengthy position (for a call option) or maybe the money needed for a corresponding brief position (for a put option) at expiration.

In case the seller does not have any ownership of the underlying asset, or maybe the corresponding funds needed for delivery of a put option, the seller will have to get it at expiration based on existing industry prices. With no protection out of the cost volatility, such roles are believed to be extremely susceptible to lose and therefore called "uncovered," or even more colloquially, "naked."

Key elements

- Naked options run the risk of big loss from fast cost change before expiration.
- Naked call options, which are exercised, develop a brief placement in the seller's account.
- Naked put options, which are exercised, build an extended position in the seller's account, bought with cash that is available.

The way a Naked Option Works

A naked job describes a circumstance where a trader offers an options contract without having a position in the underlying security as shelter from an unwanted shift of cost. Naked options are appealing to investors and traders since they have the expected volatility included in the price.

In case the basic security moves in the exact opposite direction that the option customer anticipated, or perhaps even when it moves in the buyer's favor, although not adequate to account because of the volatility pretty much built into the cost, then the seller of the option gets to keep some out-of-the-money premium. This usually would mean that option sellers win about 70% of trades. A setup that appeals to investors and traders who love to win the vast majority of their trades.

Naked Calls

A trader that creates a naked call option on a stock has recognized the obligation to promote the basic stock for the strike cost at or even before expiration, no matter exactly how high the share price rises. In case the trader doesn't wear the main stock, the seller is going to have to get the inventory, and provide the inventory to the option customer to fulfill the obligation when the option is exercised. The best outcome is the fact that this produces a short sell placement in the option sellers' accounts on the Monday after expiration. In the situation of a seller that sold a put option, the best outcome will be creating a great deal of inventory place in the option sellers' account—a place bought with money out of the option sellers' account.

For instance, imagine a trader that thinks that a stock is not likely to rise in value within the following three months, though she's not so certain that a possible decline will be huge. Believe that the inventory is valued at $100, along with a $500 strike call, with an expiration date ninety days in the long term, is being offered for $ 4.75 a share. She decides to start a naked call by "selling to open" those calls and gathering the premium. In this particular situation, she chooses not to buy the inventory since she thinks the possibility is apt to expire worthlessly, and she is going to keep the whole premium.

The possible three outcomes that are possible for a naked call trade:

Outcome #1: The Stock Rallies before Expiration

In this particular situation, the trader has a function that will be exercised. When we believe the stock rose to $130 on good earnings news, then the option is going to be excercised at $100 a share. It means that the trader should acquire the inventory at the present market price, after which promote it (or short the inventory) from $100 a share to cover her obligation. These conditions lead to a $30 per share loss ($100 - $130). There's no upper limit for just how high the inventory (and the option seller's obligations) can rise.

Outcome #2: The Stock Stays Dull Near $500 per Share at Expiration

In case the inventory is at or perhaps below the strike price at expiration, it will not be exercised, and also, the option seller gets to hold the high quality she initially collected.

Outcome #3: The Stock Has Dropped to the Cost Below $500 at Expiration.

In this particular scenario, assume the stock dropped to $90 by expiration. Generally, there will not be some customers ready to spend the strike price ($500) for a stock they can purchase on the open market for $90 a share. As in outcome #2, the choice has no value as well as the option seller gets to have the whole premium.

Naked Puts

As you have seen in the preceding results, there's simply no limit to just how high an inventory can increase; therefore, a naked call seller has theoretically limitless threat. With naked puts, on the opposite hand, seller's risk is found because a stock, or maybe some other underlying asset, may just fall to 0 dollars. A naked put option seller has recognized the obligation to purchase the underlying asset in the strike cost in case the option is exercised at or even before its expiration date. Even though the risk is contained, it can still be pretty high; therefore, brokers normally have particular rules concerning naked option trading. New traders, for instance, might not be allowed to put this order type.

Chapter 19. Options On Futures

A futures contract option gives the holder the right, but not the obligation, to purchase or sell a particular futures contract at a strike price on or before the expiry date of the option. These work in the same way as stock options, but they differ because the underlying security is a futures contract.

Many futures options, such as index options, are settled in the money. These are also European-style options, meaning that these cannot be exercised early.

How Options on Futures Work

An option for a Futures contract is similar to that for a stock option in that it allows the buyer to buy or sell the underlying asset but not to have the obligation. At the same time, they are creating a potential obligation for the salesperson to buy or sell the underlying asset if the buyer wants to exercise that option. This means the option for a futures contract or futures option is derivative security. But the price and contract characteristics of these options do not necessarily add to the leverage.

Therefore, an option for a future S&P 500 contract can be considered a second derivative of the S&P 500 index since its futures are derivatives of the index themselves. There are, therefore, more variables to be taken into account since the option and the futures contracts have expiry dates and their own supply and demand profiles. Time decay (also known as theta) functions in the same way as options in other securities, and traders have to take this factor into consideration.

The buyer of the option will enter into the long part of the contract for the call options in the future and purchase the underlying asset at the strike price of the option. With options, the option holder will enter the brief side of the contract and sell the underlying asset at the right price.

Example of Options on Futures

For an example of how such contracts work, a potential S&P 500 contract will be considered first. E-mini S&P 500 is the most common S&P 500 contract and allows an investor to manage a money amount worth 50 times the value of the S&P 500 Index. This e-mini contract will monitor the amount of $150,000 in the money should the index value be $3,000. If the index value rose by one percent to $3030, then the controlled cash would amount to $151,500. The difference here is an increase of $1,500. As this futures contract requires a margin of $6,300 (as of this letter), this change would mean a profit of 25 percent.

But rather than raise $6,300 in the money, it would be considerably cheaper to buy an option on the index. For instance, if the index costs $3,000, suppose an option for the $3,010 strike price can also be quoted at $17,00 with two weeks in advance. A buyer of this option would not be required to maintain the $6,300 margin, but would only have to pay the price of the option. This is $50 times the cost (the same multiplier as the index) of every dollar spent. This means that the option price is $850 plus commissions and fees, and around 85% less than the futures contract.

Although this option moves with the same leverage ($50 per index $1), the cash leverage used may be considerably higher. If the index rises to $3030 in a single day, as stated in the example above, the option price could go from $17.00 to $32.00. This would mean an increase in the value of $750, which would not be the profit on the futures contract alone, but would be an 88% increase instead of a 25% increase for the same amount of movements in the underlying index compared to the risks of 850$. Depending on the option to be purchased, the money traded can be leveraged or not to a greater extent than with the futures alone.

Further Considerations for Options on Futures

As stated, when assessing an option on a futures contract, there are many moving parts to consider. One of them is the fair value from the cash or the spot price of the underlying asset. The difference in the futures contract is called premium.

However, the options allow the owner, thanks to higher-margin rules (called the SPAN margin), to manage the large sums of the underlying asset with less capital. It offers additional leverage and revenues. But the profit potential leads to losses up to the full value of the contract options acquired.

The main difference between stock options and futures options is the variance in the underlying value of the stock option price. A $1 stock options change equals $1 (per share), which is uniform for all stocks. For each contract purchased, a $1 price change is worth $50 using the example of e-mini S&P 500 futures. This is not true for all futures and futures options markets. It is heavily dependent on the amount and the specifications of the goods, index, or bond defined in each futures contract.

Chapter 20. Best Demo Simulator and How to Use It

Investing in the stock market, as experts point out, requires substantial knowledge and experience to control the risk and make the appropriate decisions at the right time.

These simulators generally offer very advanced interfaces, a virtual economic fund to invest in, and real-time information. That is to say, they have all the tools and functions necessary to learn how to invest in an online stock market as if we were in the stock market itself.

Many of these computer programs belong to banks and brokers specialized in the stock market or markets such as Forex (such as Plus500). These applications— from our point of view— are more complete than the simple stock market games that we have found in the market for decades or than the apps that have overwhelmingly increased in recent years.

Most offer free demo accounts, although in some cases, we can find companies that request a small payment in exchange for using their platform. A small expense that is worth taking on and that can save us many dislikes in the future.

Why Use a Bag Simulator?

Investing in the stock market is not especially difficult, but it is essential to have good knowledge to avoid greater evils.

That is why it is essential to train previously in everything related to the markets and their operation. For this, you can go to the editorial fund of the National Commission of the Stock Market or the Madrid Stock Exchange, where we can find practical guides and handy tips for beginners and more advanced investors.

Having the advice of an expert is also a guarantee, but if you prefer to take the road alone, we recommend that you settle the bases well before playing with real money. The risk, as we have repeated, is high if it is operated without the necessary knowledge. The stock market is not a lottery that can make you rich by investing a few euros, so you should know all the mechanisms of the market entirely to understand where and when to put your money.

In this learning process, a good stock market simulator plays an essential role. With these tools, you can play with fictitious money, see how your decisions affect your income statement, and, most importantly, create solid pillars to leap to the real world of investments.

Another advantage is that the companies that offer these simulators allow you to directly operate with real money from the same or a similar platform, so you will already be familiar with the interface. In many cases, it is only necessary to convert your demo account into a real account and make an income, without changing the program.

Pay for a Bag Simulator?

Many people are wondering what the best free bag simulator for beginners is. It is true that in the market, we can find compelling tools that do not require the payment of any amount, but it is also true that skimping on this section can be a real mistake.

Creating a CFD bag simulator that offers guarantees entails a considerable programming expense and high operating costs. That is why some companies ask for a small subscription in exchange for their use that does not usually reach 10 euros per month. A minimum amount for a tool that tells you how to learn to invest in the stock market from home, and that allows you to practice with all the guarantees; it's worth it by any standards, of course.

Also, it is widespread that with that small fee, the user has access to manuals, tutorials, webinars, and other teaching materials to support the practical part with theoretical foundations. Investing in the stock market in the short term is not recommended, so all this material can be of high relevance to fix concepts.

The Best Bag Simulators

Once this preamble has been completed, we will analyze five of the most exciting simulators in the market. All are backed by companies with ample experience in the sector (they are banks or brokers) and are well above in quality and performance of simple stock games (we do not recommend using these games as part of your training). This listing is sorted alphabetically.

Active Trade

This real-time stock market simulator offers users an account with 100,000 virtual euros so they can practice without fear of losing their money. It has personalized support and, most importantly, courses and trading programs taught by professional traders.

With this tool, you can create your strategy, control your investments, find the companies that best fit your profile, and get detailed information on more than 18,400 shares—essential functions to create your profile as an investor and locate those opportunities that you can take advantage of in the real world.

IG Spain

The demo account of this stock market simulator allows you to invest in an online stock market in a risk-free environment. This free account has a virtual fund of 20,000 euros and offers graphics and prices in real-time. Also, you can check from your mobile or tablet to continue operating anywhere, even if you don't have a computer. The interface can be customized to suit your tastes and your style.

This demo account, however, does not offer all the functionality of the real platform. The most notable differences are the following:

- Transactions made through the demo account are not subject to slippage, interest or dividend adjustments, or price movements out of the negotiation.
- Transactions can be rejected if you do not have enough funds to open them, but they will not be denied due to size or price issues.
- The graphics packages have no cost.
- The positions will not be closed if you do not have enough funds to cover the margin or current losses, something that does happen in a real account.

Orey iTrade

Another easy-to-use bag simulator is Orey iTrade. With this tool, you will learn to invest in both the Spanish selective, that is, in the IBEX 35, as in other critical global exchanges—all online and free, since you can try it without cost and obligation.

Through its interface, you can access stock quotes in real-time and different analyses, comparative, and graphical tools. The account begins with a virtual fund of 100,000 euros to start investing.

Société Générale

This trading simulator seems to us one of the most interesting since it will allow you to delve into the world of warrants, something that is not available in most of the free tools. The simulator of this French bank makes available to its users 10,000 fictitious euros to negotiate on the listed products of Société Générale and test their investment strategy without risk.

To start operating, you must register on the website www.sgbolsa.es. Registration is free. Also, the entity usually raffles gifts such as mobile phones or tablets among its new users, one more argument to try the Market Simulator, as they call it.

To use the system, follow these steps:

- Register on the website www.Warrants.com.
- Connect to the website www.Warrants.com or the simulator using the e-mail and the registration password.
- Access the simulator from the Tools menu of the website www.Warrants.com.

TraderTwit

The TraderTwit simulator catches our attention since it has enormous educational value. It is not free (although it is cheap), but instead offers training and a compelling platform. They have a lot of news from the sector, an exciting collaborative platform, and thousands of interactive analyses.

We like what they call "the challenge." It is something like a 50-level training program that puts users in challenges to move from level to level. In each of them, you have to follow instructions, such as the maximum lever that can be used or the maximum loss streak. There are also objectives to be achieved.

Based on these criteria, the user can carry out operations of buying and selling currencies, indices, or raw materials—an excellent way to learn while having fun and competing against other users in the community. Also, the best usually takes real prizes.

Chapter 21. Options Trading Jargon

Every industry has its own specialized lingo, and options trading is no exception. Let's give a quick overview that will help you understand when reading about options and help you navigate the markets effectively.

Ask

The price that a seller is asking for security, or put another way, the smallest price a seller is willing to accept to sell it.

Assignment

When the buyer of an options contract exercises their option, a notice is sent to the seller. The seller is then obligated to dispose of (in the case of a call) or purchase (in the case of a put) stocks at the strike price.

At the Money

This means that the current market price is equal to the strike price.

Bear Call Spread

The bear call spread (also known as call credit spread) is a bearish to neutral options trading vertical spread strategy. The position is composed of a short and a long call having the same underlying, same expiration date, and different strike prices.

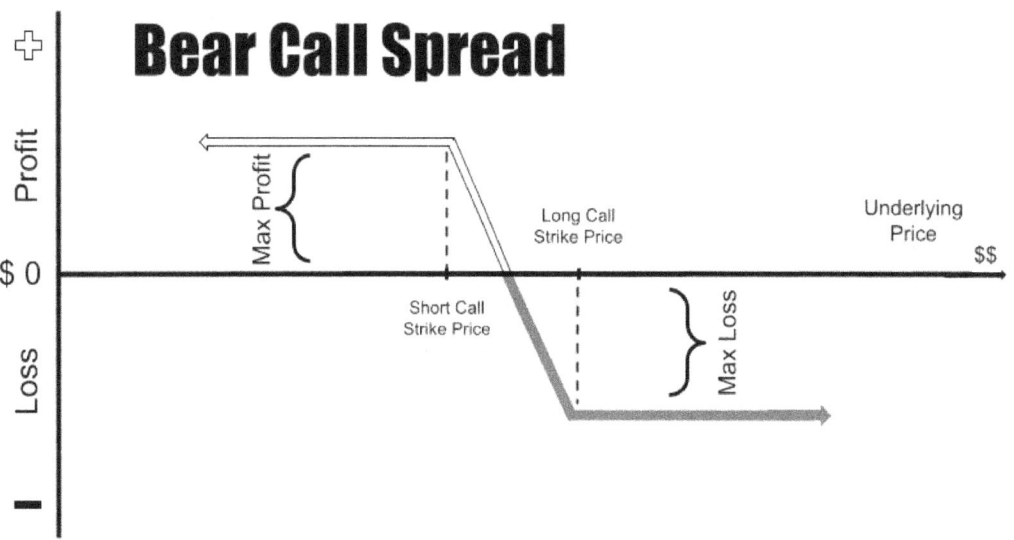

Bid Price

This term refers to the optimum amount that a dealer is willing to shell out for the security.

Break-Even Point

When neither a profit nor a loss have been realized.

Bull Put Spread

The bull put spread (also known as put credit spread) is a bullish to neutral options trading vertical spread strategy. The position is composed of a short and a long put having the same underlying, same expiration date, and different strike prices.

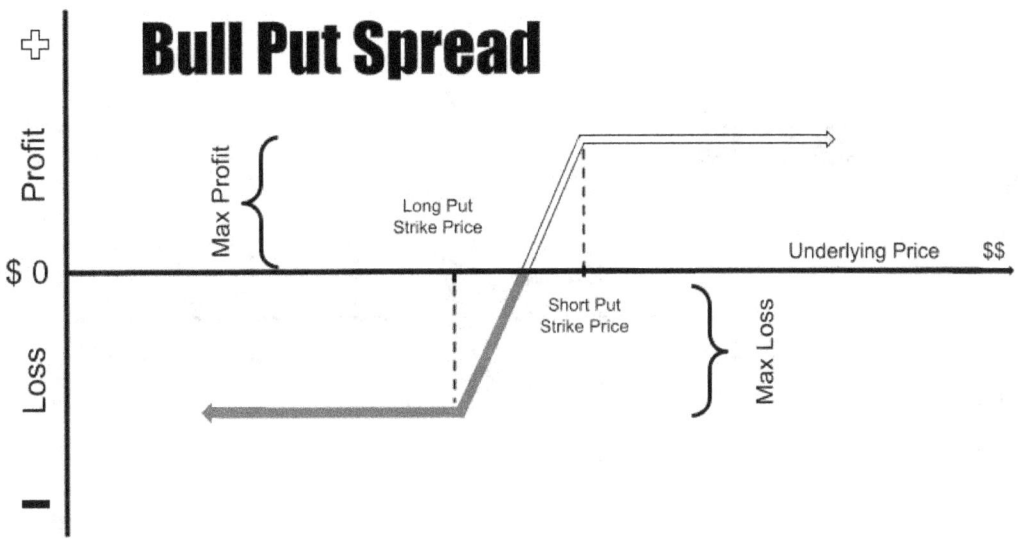

Call (Long Call)

The buyer of a call option has the right to buy 100 shares of a stock at the strike price at any time before the options contract expires. This is an option, so the buyer does not have to buy the shares. The seller of a call contract must buy the shares under any circumstances up to the expiration of the contract if the buyer exercises their right before the contract expires.

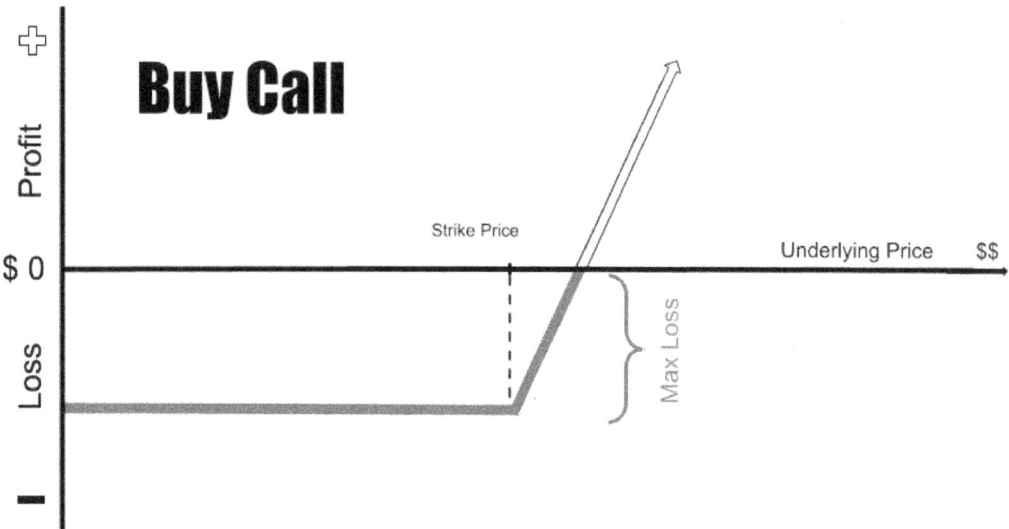

Commission

A fee charged by a brokerage firm to execute an option order on an exchange.

Delta

If the underlying stock changes by a point in value, the delta is the change in the value of the option.

Early Exercise

If an options contract is exercised before the expiration date, it is said to be early.

Exercise

The buyer of the option exercises their right to buy stock for a call or sell the stock for a put.

84

Expiration Date

Options contracts expire on the third Friday of every month. When you see an option quote such as:

JUN 70

That means that the option expires on the third Friday in June, with a strike price of $70.

In the Money (Call)

This refers to the occurrence of when the current market price exceeds the strike price. This is the gross profit per share (not including premium and other fees).

In the Money (Put)

For a put contract, it is in-the-money when the current stock price is less than the strike price.

Index Options

An index option doesn't have individual stocks as the underlying. Instead the underlying is an index like the NASDAQ. An index option can't be exercised until the expiry date.

Intrinsic Value

An apt example would be: if the current price is at $10, then the market price is at $20, the intrinsic value would be $10. If the current price were $25, the intrinsic value would be $15.

Iron Condor

An iron condor is a combo of combo positions. It is composed of a bull put spread and a bear call spread. Iron condors have two break-even points, and it is useful when the underlying is expected to remains within a given range until the options expiration date. It offers limited profit as well as limited risk.

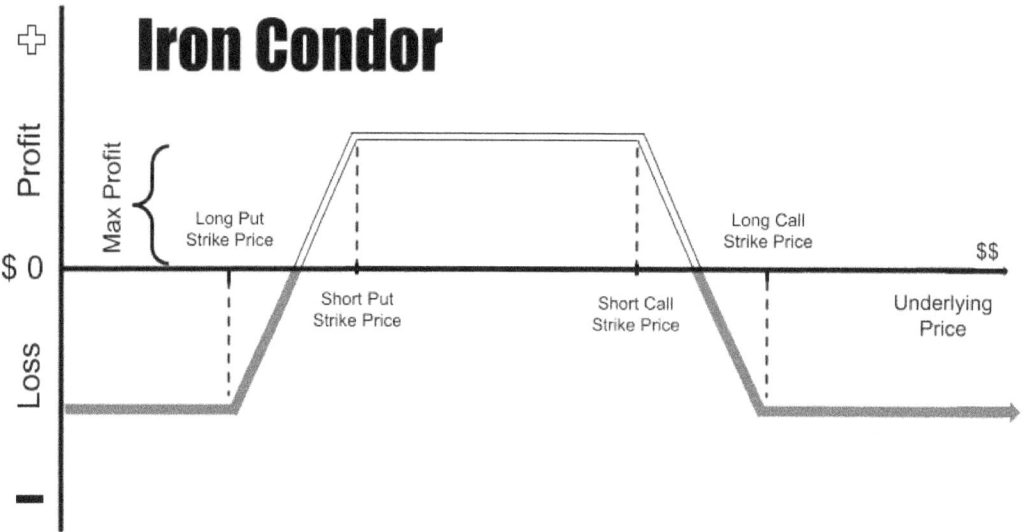

Leap

A LEAP is a long-term equity anticipation security. Basically, these are long-term options contracts. LEAP contracts can last as long as three years. LEAPS are generally more expensive than most options, because of the longtime value which gives them more time to be "in the money."

Legs

A leg is one part of a position when there are two or more options or positions in the underlying stock.

Long

Long means ownership when it is held in your account. You can be long on a stock or an option.

Margin Requirement

If you are selling options, you will be required to deposit some cash with the brokerage to cover your positions. In other words, it is cash in your account for the brokerage to buy or sell shares as required by your obligations in the options contract.

Option Chain

An option chain is something you'll look at when viewing available options online. It's basically a table for the options available for a given underlying stock. For a given expiration date, the option chain will include all puts and calls, and strike prices that are available.

Premium

This is the price paid per share for an options contract. Since the contract has 100 shares, the price paid, or the total premium is 100 times the premium. The seller is able to keep the premium regardless of whether or not the buyer exercises their options.

Put

The buyer of a put option has the right to sell 100 shares at the strike price on or before the expiry date.

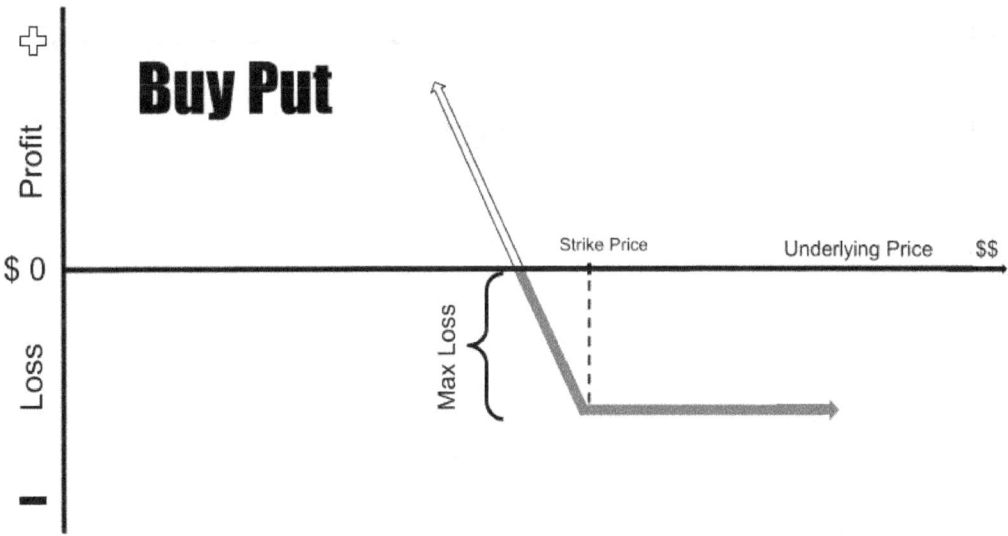

Roll a Long Position

Rolling a long position means to sell options and then acquire others with the same underlying stock but with different strike prices and expiration dates.

Roll a Short Position

Rolling a short position means buying to close an existing position and selling for the purposes of opening new positions with different strike prices and expiration dates "rolled out" in time.

Sell Call (Short Call)

The seller of a call option has the duty to delivery 100 shares at the strike price on or before the expiry date, if the buyer requires them.

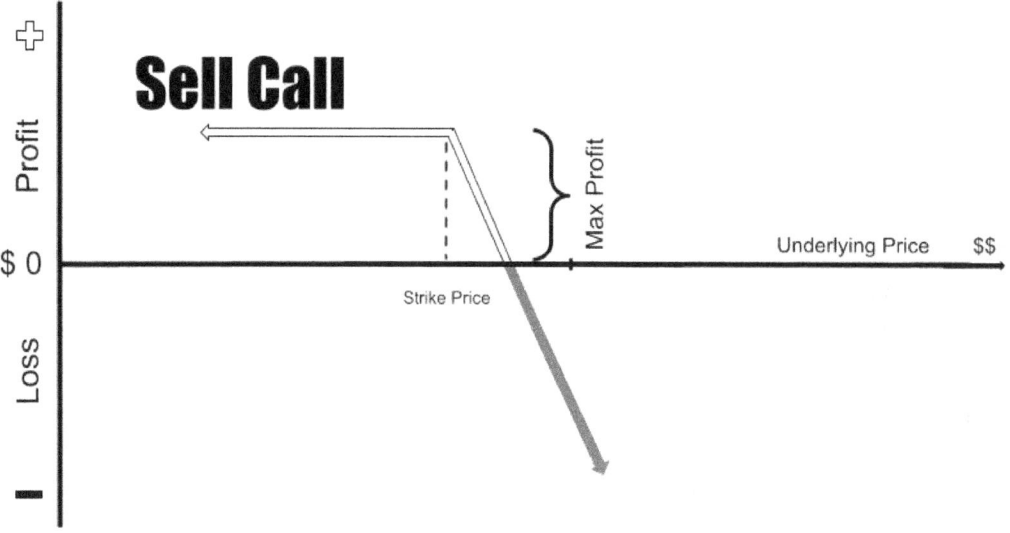

Sell Put (Short Put)

The seller of a put option has the duty to delivery 100 shares at the strike price on or before the expiry date, if the buyer requires them.

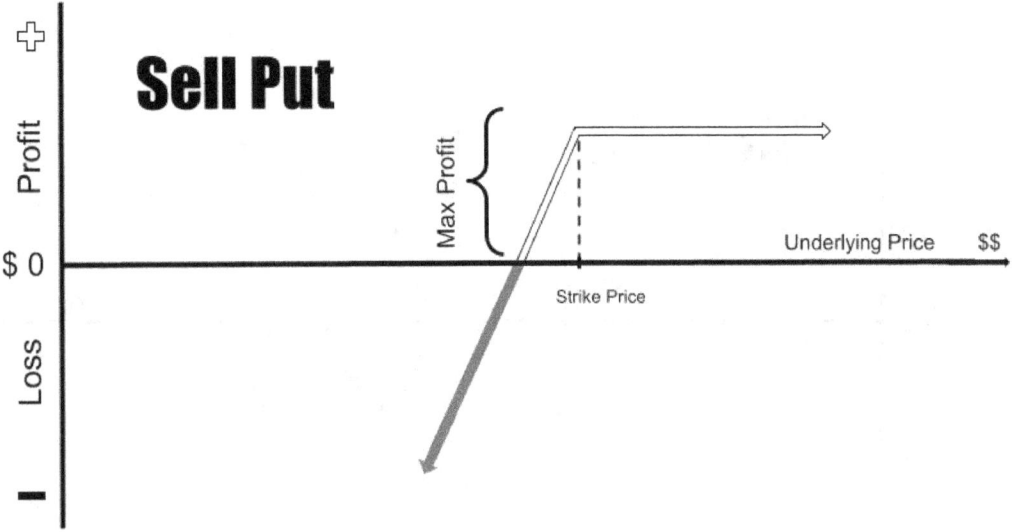

Series

Options are grouped together in series on the markets. Options in the same series can be calls or puts, but they have the same expiration date and strike price.

Short

Selling a security that you don't actually own.

Straddle

A straddle is a "combo" position consisting of a Long Call and a Long Put having the same strike and expiration date. A straddle is useful when a strong movement is expected by the underlying within a short period, before the options expiration date.

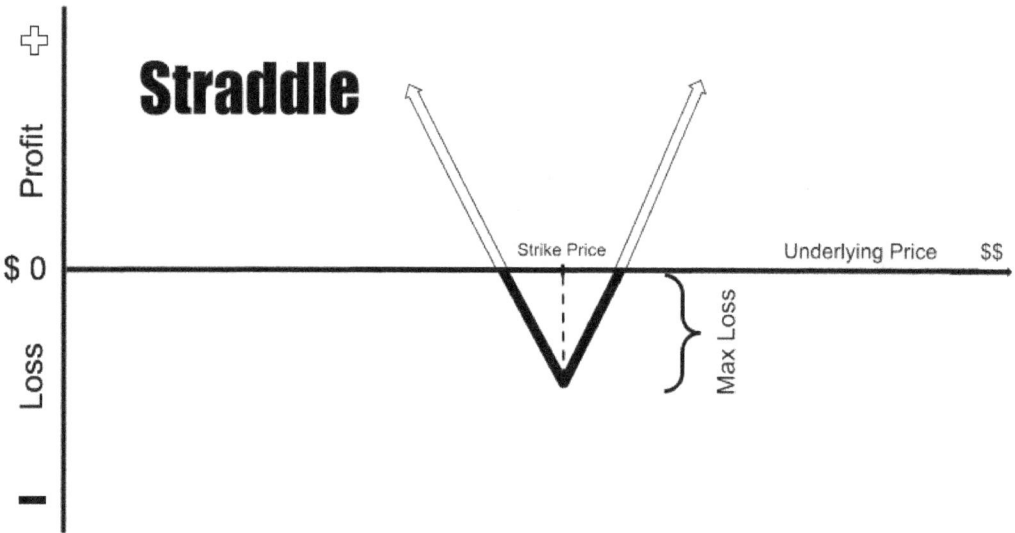

Strike Price

It is the amount per share of the agreed upon contract. If the option to buy or sell is exercised by the purchaser of an options contract, the shares must be bought or sold at the strike price. When you look at options online, the strike price is given at the end of the options symbol. For example, you might see:

00040000

The decimal point is found by moving three places from the right. So, this represents a strike price of $40. On the other hand:

00005600

It would represent a strike price of $5.60.

Time Value

How long it's left until an options contract expires. Generally, more time value will mean that an option is worth more when trading. The reason is that the more time until the option expires, the more chance there is for the underlying stock to beat the strike price. In the case of a call option, that means going above the strike price, while in the case of a put option, that means going below the strike price. What investors are looking for is enough time value for an option to be in the money.

Time Decay

Time decay is simply a measure of the decrease in the time value of an options contract.

Underlying

The underlying stock is the specific stock that the option contract is based on. This is the stock that is actually traded if the option is exercised.

Vertical Spread

Vertical Spreads are combo positions that offer limited risks as well as limited potential profits. It is a result of combined short and long options with different strikes and the same expiration date (see Bear Call Spread and Bull Put Spread).

Weekly

A weekly is a kind of option that expires within a week, rather than a monthly time frame. Since weeklies have a short time value, they are cheaper, but the risks involved are higher. Investors who like weeklies are hoping to capitalize on an option that tightly fits a given date coming up in the near future. Weeklies usually expire on Friday afternoons at market close. Weeklies help traders that are trying to exploit short-term events for profits. For example, investors might target an earnings report or an anticipated product announcement.

Conclusion

In this final post of the Options Trading Crash Course, we're going to take a look at some additional trading strategies. We'll start with the one that might be less familiar: spreads. A spread is an options strategy where the trader buys and sells options of the same type (i.e. two call spreads, two put spreads, etc.), but with different strike prices or expiration dates.

As you might imagine, spreads have the potential to decrease the risk of your options trades, while simultaneously increasing your profit potential. There are two types of spreads that we'll cover in this post: credit spreads and debit spreads. Credit spreads are trades where the options trader receives money upfront to enter into the trade.

Debit spreads, on the other hand, are trades where the options trader has to part with some of their own capital in order to enter into the trade.

Let's begin with credit spreads.

This money can either be a rebate from the option premium or a "premium credit" from another options trade. Let's imagine that you purchase an at-the-money call option on XYZ stock with a strike price of 50.

This option currently has an implied volatility of 30%. Shortly after you purchase the call option, XYZ stock experiences a large price increase to $52 per share. If the implied volatility of the option you purchased has not changed, then your call option would be worth $4.50 per share. This means that you would have a credit of $4. This $4 is the amount of profit you would earn from your credit spread. Since you have a credit spread, you make money when the stock moves in either direction. If the stock rises in price, you make money on the call option you bought. If the stock decreases in price, you still make money since the option's premium will decrease. You can even have a credit spread on an option that expires worthless. In this case, the credit you receive is considered to be intrinsic value.

Now let's look at debit spreads.

Debit spreads are trades where the options trader has to part with some of their own capital in order to enter into the trade. Debit spreads are trades where the options trader has to part with some of their own capital in order to enter into the trade.

A crash course in options trading is now at your fingertips. It is an easy way of maximizing profit while limiting risk. The more you trade, the better you will get at it and the more successful you will be.

On the first trading day of each month, the market will be open for trading as usual. On the last day of the month, the market will be closed for trading. There is no need to sit for long hours. The crash course requires less time. You will also be able to make better decisions because of the information you have at your fingertips. Investing in the markets can be a very rewarding experience.

The knowledge that you gain from this course will give you the edge when it comes to investing. You will be able to make money in all market conditions by trading options. So, invest and invest wisely. This crash course in options trading is your ticket to making a lot of money.